DON'T WAIT TO BE RESCUED

Transcending the Death
Experience

by

Shirley Pratt

A Lohr Publication

ODYSSEY PRESS INC.
DOVER, NEW HAMPSHIRE 03820

Send inquiries, or orders (with $1
for postage) to:
A LOHR Publication
P.O. Box 587
Needham, MA 02192

Library of Congress Catalog Card Number:
91-90036

ISBN 0-9628951-0-5

Dedicated to my first partner, Dorothy Stoddart.

Missed by all.

Acknowledgments

I wish to thank my husband, Bob, for putting up with my lack of computer knowledge, and helping me to straighten out many a frustrating moment. I wish to thank my son, Russell, for his work on my page layout. I wish to thank Kathryn Exon for checking my punctuation. It ranks in the same category as computers. And a very special thank you to Dr. Glen W. Snowden for all the guidance he gave me in making my manuscript more comprehensible.

Contents

I   Crossing Them Over............................1

II   My Guide, Mary................................21

III   Hanging Around..............................27

IV   Suicide 47

V   How The Spirits Find Us 53

VI   Quite A Variety...............................73

VII The Continuing Experience 93

VIII Ghosts..105

IX   Time To Cross Over..........................123

X   Saying Your Goodbyes......................133

XI   The Welcome...................................141

XII The Spirit Plane...............................147

Introduction

It may be difficult for some people to understand what Rescues are all about. If you have never heard about Rescues, I hope that you will be sympathetic to my endeavors and remember my message when it is your time to cross over to the spiritual plane. If you have heard about Rescues, I hope that my experiences will give you a greater understanding.

Everything in this book is based on my own personal experiences and those of my partners, except in the few instances when I refer to testimony given by others and incorporated into other books. I have seldom heard the subject of Rescues discussed by anyone else and wonder just how many people are actually doing them. But I have heard Dr. Raymond Moody, Jr. speak, and I have also read and heard about personal near-death experiences. They are not the same thing at all, and not to be confused with Rescuing the human spirit if it has not crossed over.

Many of the interviews in this book are not complete. The spirits all crossed over, but only the pertinent part relating to the subject of the chapter is presented in many instances. The exceptions either have a very interesting story or show an example to prove a point.

All names have been changed except those of famous people.

The reader will notice, as they proceed through the book, that sometimes I will refer to the spirit as "it", and other times the spirit will be called "he" or "she". I often think of the spirits we are working with as actual people, and therefore, sometimes have a problem deciding how to refer to them. Thus, my inconsistency.

This is my personal message to the world, and I hope that everyone who reads this book will be inspired enough to follow my suggestion and cross over to the spiritual plane when they die.

Shirley Pratt

CHAPTER I

Crossing Them Over

"Cross over, cross over," is the message I send mentally every time I see or hear about the death of a person, or a group of persons, on the television or the radio. "Don't wait to be Rescued," I instruct them.

My reaction is instant, as I have often thought of all the spirits out there, hanging around, who have not crossed over to the spiritual plane and are stuck on the earthly plane until someone is able to Rescue them.

I mentally send out the message that if they don't cross over when they die, or at the time of their funeral, they won't be able to cross over later on without special help. This is what I've been told by my spirit guides. It's important that the spirits of those who have died receive this message, but I honestly don't know if they usually do or not. After giving out my message, I just hope, and then go on about my business.

Since I have been told that thoughts are energy, and that all energy goes out and can be picked up by anyone in spirit, I just assume that they get my message and use it if they so desire.

When I began doing Rescues with Dot, my first partner, I had no idea there were so many spirits out there who hadn't crossed over. Since I have now helped thousands to cross over, I know that there must be hundreds of thousands, or millions of spirits, just waiting for a chance to go to the spiritual plane. Or perhaps they are just lost in space and have no idea what to do.

Crossing over, from the earthly plane to the spiritual plane (also referred to as heaven), is the natural procedure for spirits at the time of the death of the physical body. It is unusual for the spirit to hang around after the body has died. And, if the spirit hangs around for too long a period of time after death, then it won't be able to cross over without help.

The point we try to make, to any spirit who isn't too willing to be Rescued, is that once it does cross over, it can go back and forth between the spiritual plane and the earthly plane as often as it likes.

Mediums, and others who are able, should take the time to do more Rescues. Although there isn't any monetary gain, there certainly is spiritual satisfaction. Those who know how to do this would be of immeasurable help to all those spirits who wish to cross over and haven't been able to do so. It is simply impossible for those of us who are doing this on a regular basis to cross over all who desire to go.

Not every spirit feels confident about crossing over at the time of death. One day when Dot was on her way to my house, she passed a church where a funeral was taking place. When Dot arrived she told me about the funeral and how, as she had passed the church, she had thought about the person who was being eulogized. That person had been well known in town. Well, right in the middle of doing Rescues, that particular spirit came through me and asked to be crossed over. Dot tried to ask him some questions, but he said, "Hurry up! I want to get back to my funeral." He didn't want to take any chances. He just wanted to make doubly sure that he crossed over!

Dot and I, as partners, were able to cross over more than eight hundred spirits in the three and one-half years that we did Rescues, but this was on the basis of one at a time. It would take us anywhere from ten minutes to half an hour to cross each individual spirit over. Once in a great while we have spirits who are extremely slow about crossing because they either wanted to tell us their entire life history, or were simply afraid of what they would find when they did cross over. We always made a point of crossing over at least six spirits each time we got together to do Rescues, and that was once a week. So, you can see that it took years just to cross a few hundred over.

And that doesn't even take into consideration those spirits we considered ghosts. It always took us several tries before we could convince a ghost to cross over. Ghosts always seemed to us to be unhappy spirits who enjoyed bothering people here on earth. They just didn't want to cross over.

One day Dot asked my guide, Mary, "Is it possible to get some of these lost souls Rescued by just directing them to look for the light and go toward it?"

"No. That's why you have to write the book."

"Do you think we could get more people to do this if we

write a book?"

"You'll get more people to go when they die," Mary answered. "A lot of people don't want to die."

"So it will prevent this backlog jam here?"

"I hope so," replied Mary.

"I hope so, too," echoed Dot.

"I can't predict. Many people have tried," Mary said. "Many spirits have tried to cross over by themselves."

I've already mentioned this but it seems important to put this exact conversation in as reinforcement of the idea that it is necessary to cross over at the time of death.

I had often wondered if there was a way we could cross these spirits over in groups. We were only crossing them over one at a time, which meant that we were only able to help six or eight each week.

When Dot died, I became frustrated at the thought that I wouldn't be able to do Rescues unless I could find someone to help me. But I also wanted to be able to cross over groups of spirits. I had thought about this for some time. So I asked my guides if it were possible to cross spirits over in groups and was given the answer that I would be told the procedure.

Well, I did find a temporary new partner in Ernie, and after she tried doing a few Rescues with me, we were told how we could Rescue a group of spirits all at once instead of just being able to do one Rescue at a time.

My guide, Mary, told us to "just tell the spirits to hold

hands when they're ready to cross over." So, when Rufus came to be crossed over, Ernie and I decided to try the new instructions.

Ernie told him, "Now listen, Rufus, we're going to try something today. We're going to try to cross everybody over together."

"I heard that," Rufus said, meaning he had heard Mary explain this to Ernie and me.

"We're going to ask everybody here who is within reach of the voice to hold hands."

"What am I going to do here?" Rufus inquired.

"You're going to hold hands with everybody, and would you like to be the spokesman for the group?"

"Well, I don't know. I'm here now...do I have to leave?"

"No, you stay right here, but just ask if there are any other souls around who want to cross over."

"Oh, yes!" Rufus exclaimed. "There's a great many here."

"All right, everybody hold hands," Ernie instructed. "Are you all holding hands now?"

Rufus said they all wanted to tell their names. The other spirits identified themselves to Rufus, who then repeated the names to Ernie. She acknowledged each one of them, and as she did, her hands became very heavy because so many spirits were holding hands.

When the spirit of Rufus was ready to cross over, Ernie made certain that the other spirits were ready also, and they all crossed over together.

Dot and I used to hold hands, as one of us acted as the medium for the spirit to come through, and we could always feel a tingling. But with the spirits now crossing in groups, my hands and those of my partner feel much heavier and the tingling can be much stronger.

It's really exciting to think that it's possible to cross over so many spirits in so short a time. Now everyone who wishes to go can join hands and we can cross them over together.

Since then we have crossed many groups and found that there can be quite a variety in each group. There really is no such thing as a typical group.

Homer told Ernie that he was a ninety-one year old farmer from Indiana. "I came because I heard Shirley talking about Indiana yesterday."

After he had talked about himself, Ernie told him, "Look and see if you see anyone."

"Humph. I can't believe this one. This one (meaning the first person in line next to him) is dressed like Donald Duck and says that he's a Walt Disney character. What kind of joke is that?" he laughed. "He said that he used to draw for Walt Disney, so this is the way he wants to look. Well, to each his own, they say."

"Are there any more?" Ernie asked.

"There's a boy and girl here. Well, they were in a boating accident—they were sailing in a sailboat. "Oh, oh, wait a minute. Wait a minute. My mother told me about things like this and I heard about them in school—a covered wagon? There's a covered wagon that's coming right up and there's a lot of people getting out. They're just getting out to show me they're here and they're getting back in again. 'The Oregon Trail' they said, and they were attacked by Indians. Oh, there's another covered wagon. I think I should ask them how many want to go. There's seventeen of them."

Ernie had them all hold hands and all twenty-one spirits crossed over together.

We have a special procedure as taught me by my guide. The spirit comes through me and goes through the usual interview, identifying him or herself, the year, place and anything else they want to talk about.

Then, when they are ready to cross over, my partner asks if they would look to see if there are any other spirits, to their right, who might want to be crossed over with them. There are always other spirits waiting to go. So, the spirit my partner is interviewing informs my partner who each additional spirit is. Quite often he or she describes what they are wearing and what they are doing. If he is told anything by the other spirits, he also gives my partner this information.

Sometimes the spirit to be Rescued can see the other spirits quite clearly, and therefore, so can I. The spirit in me will describe what it is seeing. Then, when the spirit in me is ready to cross over it will ask the other spirits, who are waiting, if they are ready to go also. No one crosses until they are all seeing the bright light of the spirits who have come to help each of them cross over. They all cross over en masse.

Sometimes there will only be as few as four crossing over together and sometimes there will be as many as twenty or sixty. After the Armenian earthquake there were five hundred!

Ruth, my new partner, and I were doing Rescues on December 14, 1988, when Stefan came through me shouting, "They could have gotten us out!"

"Where are you?" asked Ruth.

"Armenia."

"Are you alive down below?"

The spirit shook my head. "We called. We called," he said, as he began to cry. "Why did they take so long?"

"Where were you?"

"I was home. I was ill. My children were in school.

"I don't know why!" he cried out. "My wife had gone to work."

Stefan was crying. "There's many here. There's many! There's many. Oh, they should have—why didn't they—"

"Shirley and I can help you cross over."

"Yes," he replied. "She kept saying, 'Cross over.'"

Continuing to cry, Stefan complained to Ruth, "Oh, my chest was crushed. Oh, it was painful. I can feel it still. There are others here with me."

"I know there are."

Then Ruth tried to tell the group to hold hands, but Stefan was in such agonizing grief that he really didn't hear her.

"There's about fifteen with me here now. We were all waiting...why couldn't they have gotten us? We could hear them!"

"Stefan, I know. It's a sad, sad thing. The whole world is upset. This country has sent money, material and clothes, but it didn't get there in time. I think it's the winter weather. It was so terrible."

"No," Stefan answered defiantly, "the Russians don't know how to do anything. We don't like them. Some of us hate them. They don't like us to be Armenians! They don't like our religion."

Ruth tried to sound convincing. "But there is hope. Gorbachev—"

"Oh, we don't believe him. He's just saying that for the world."

"I think he's a good man."

"They took our country. Everyone, everyone— everyone tried to steal it from us." Stefan cried again. "I don't know. I don't know," he said.

"It's terribly sad. It's terribly sad," Ruth said, feeling like crying herself.

"I want to go."

"Someone will come for you."

"My parents are here. I don't know where Maya and the children are. Oh, my Maya's here. Oh, that means she died, too. Where are my children?" he cried out.

"Everything will be fine," Ruth said, trying to comfort him.

"Do not believe the Russians. We do not trust them. WE ARE NOT RUSSIA. WE ARE ARMENIA!" Stefan shouted as he crossed over.

I got the feeling that more spirits were waiting to come through, and one in particular seemed to be thinking about what could be done there in Armenia.

Immediately Gregor came through me. "What we all do about this?" he asked.

"When did you die?" Ruth inquired.

"Died when it happened. There are so many, and they are frightened, and they do not wish to leave because they are searching themselves. They are searching for their loved ones. What we all do about this?"

"Could you tell me your name first?"

"Yes, my name is Gregor. I hear you say that—you call Stefan by this name. You say Gregor."

"Yes," Ruth agreed, as she had indeed accidently called Stefan by the name of Gregor.

"You say Gregor and I hear you and I come."

"I am Russian, not Armenian," Gregor explained, "but I live there. I Russian official."

"Oh, you are? You have a little different accent."

"Yes."

"You died in the terrible—"

"Yes. I'm in charge or I was in charge of what you would call police."

"Of course. Well, there were political troubles there."

"Yes, but we not know this! What to do. We not know."

Ruth then explained that we would cross him over, but he protested. "We must be here. We must help. We have work to do. We do not know what to do! We do not wish to leave."

"It would be more help to go over. You could then give help to people's minds."

"How could we do that?"

"You can inspire them."

"Could we come? Could we be here?"

"Yes!"

"Can we be here after we go?"

"Yes."

"We wish to."

"Are there many people with you?" Ruth inquired.

"Many. Five hundred."

"Oh, my! The whole world is full of sympathy for what has happened. It's the biggest disaster to hit the whole world. Even former enemies are sending help."

"Who are they?"

"The cold war enemies...so that work would be done. You're not expected to do that work anymore.

"So, tell the people to hold hands," Ruth instructed.

"We not know what to do!" Gregor protested. "That why we not leave."

Ruth told him what to do, and he asked, "Can we all go?

We are able?"

"Yes, yes," she assured him.

"We all wish to go."

Ruth explained the procedure again.

"My poppa," Gregor announced, meaning his poppa, who was in spirit, had come to take him across. Then he waited for the others to be ready to cross over, also.

As soon as he left, Shirley knew another spirit was with her who wanted to be Rescued.

"Hello," Ruth said.

"Oh, God, it's about time!"

"Could you tell me your name?"

"Denise."

"When did you live?"

"I just died—just died!"

"Oh, really. In what part of the world?"

"I was in Armenia."

"You were? Were you a tourist? Were you a visitor?"

"A visitor. I was with my friend," Denise explained, "and we were on our way to see her family."

"Was she Armenian?"

"Yes. Her name was Adriane."

"Did she die, too?" Ruth wondered.

"I don't know what happened to her.

"I have the feeling I was at a train station."

"Are you from America?"

"I was from this country, but my mother was from Armenia. I was trying to trace her family. My mother died when I was younger...there's Armenians here."

"Yes, yes. Are there others with you?" Ruth asked.

"You mean that died?"

"Yes."

"It was terrible. Oh—yes, there's a lot!"

Ruth was feeling very sympathic and sad. "Oh. Oh, well, tell them, Denise, tell them, Denise, to hold hands, and this is for you, too. Tell them to hold hands. And tell them that they can come back to the earth to visit once they cross over. And you'll be much, much more comfortable once you cross over.

"How many are there?" Ruth questioned.

"They're like milling around."

"Oh, they are?"

"They're confused," Denise reported as she began to cough. "I'm cold." I, myself, began to feel cold, as I can feel what the spirit feels. "Oh, it's cold," she whispered.

"I know," said Ruth. "That was part of the trouble. The rescue workers—were delayed because of the cold."

"Bunch of fools!" Denise snapped.

"Are they holding hands and ready to go?"

"Yes, they're ready."

Ruth took her through the process of crossing over.

"Oh, I'm tired, so tired.

"Where are we going?"

"To a place called heaven...you can still come back and help your loved ones, if you want," Ruth said. She meant that the loved one would have a comforting feeling when the spirit was around if it had crossed over.

"I'm very cold. I wish I had a blanket...I'm cold, so cold. I don't know if I'm dead or alive. I'm so cold." And at that point Denise's brother came and helped her to cross over.

The five hundred still hadn't crossed over. My guide, Mary, came and said that they hadn't been Rescued and that it might have been too much for Denise to have them go with her as "she was having enough trouble dealing with her pains. It might have been too much for her...she didn't think she was dead...she's not right here. She might have crossed over." We certainly hoped so.

As soon as Mary left, a spirit who was having a coughing spell came through me and said, "Oh, it's dusty."

"I know, I know, " said Ruth. "It's been a terrible earthquake.

"You're from Armenia, aren't you?"

"Yes."

"Can you tell me your name?"

"We're ready to go," the spirit whispered as she continued to cough, and Ruth and I knew that she was referring to the five hundred spirits who were trying to cross over.

"All hold hands," Ruth instructed. "Someone will come for you from heaven. The light will get brighter and stronger."

"Do you want to know my name?" the spirit whispered.

"Yes, I do," Ruth replied.

"Well, to say it like you speak it would be Mariaan."

"Mariaan."

"I am seventy."

"Tell the people—"

"Yes, there are many of them."

"Tell the people to hold hands and someone who loves you—"

"We wish to go to God," Mariaan interrupted.

"Oh, course! Someone will come in the light and take you there," Ruth told her.

"I always wear my cross and it is not with me."

"Well, you are wearing it in your heart."

"We are all to go! We are all going together. I will not go if the rest cannot."

"We'll wait," Ruth assured her.

"My family's all here—everyone."

"You let me know when they're all ready to go."

"The angels have come for us. Oh, the angels have come for us!"

"Oh, I'm so glad. I'm so glad!" Ruth cried with joy.

Ruth and I felt, like we have many times since, that we were right there when history was being made.

After the Armenians had been Rescued, Mary, my guide, came through me and explained to Ruth what had happened. Since Ruth had only been doing Rescues for a few weeks, Mary probably felt that crossing such a large group needed some explanation.

"That's quite a project!" Mary said. "But to get all these souls together ready to cross—"

"Of course, of course."

"Usually we have a line," Mary continued, "and a few go at a time. But when there's a group and the group all died together then quite often they want to go together.

"Now, we have had more large groups," Mary explained. "We have had British regiments, but we usually do not know the number of spirits in these. They have been together as regiments. They have been together for quite a period of time after they died, whereas the Armenians have just been so recent, in death, that these poor souls are still quite confused, and do not feel the cohesiveness of the regiment members. People who have died in plane crashes or ship sinkings have usually felt this same cohesiveness and have all crossed over together."

We noted that to be true when we had the captain and the entire crew from the ship *Goodfellow* come to be Rescued. They were returning to England, from a voyage to Borneo, when their ship sank during a storm in the Indian Ocean. They had stayed together as a group, and not crossed over, for over one hundred years because at least one of them didn't want to cross over.

The captain said, "We're all together. We've been together for a long time...some of them couldn't accept it...death, I mean."

Thank goodness for my guide, Mary. She is able to explain

all our questions and many that we do not even think of asking.

For some time I had been curious about the fact that we had not Rescued anyone earlier than the tenth century. Where were the spirits of those who had died previous to that time and not crossed over? I asked my guides what would happen to the spirit if the body died and the spirit didn't cross over. I was told that eventually the "spirit will dissipate into the universe." That seemed very sad and I decided that I would try to Rescue even more spirits.

Since then we have had just one spirit of a period earlier than the tenth century. His name was Aranamus and he seemed like a very special spirit—he was an exception.

"I think I come from far away," he said in a very faint voice.

Sensing that it was actually a very distant time period, Ruth asked, "A long time ago, maybe? Can you tell me what year it is? What you last remember?"

"You are right. It is a long time."

Ruth persisted. "What is the last year you remember?"

"I saw him on the cross."

"You did! You did! Oh, my. Can you tell me your name?"

"Aranamus...a Roman soldier...I thought they were wrong—to do it to him."

"Did you speak out?" Ruth asked.

"I would have been killed if I had spoken. You do not say anything. You do not say anything even when you are not on duty."

"I see. I see."

"They killed the Christ."

"But did you know he still lives? The spirit still lives!" Ruth emphasized. "They couldn't kill that."

"All spirits live, but they shouldn't have done it."

"Why have you waited so long?" Ruth inquired.

"They needed a reason...the people were so happy with him.

"I see him on the cross. I see them on the crosses."

"The three crosses?" Ruth questioned.

"The men only. I was one of the guards...at the foot of the hill."

"Oh, dear. And this bothered you all of these years, is that right?"

"Yes."

"Do you know what year it is now?"

"No."

"Almost two thousand years have gone by."

"I heard a voice call out, 'God'."

"Just now?" Ruth asked.

"Here, yes."

"Oh, yes. It was a man who died," Ruth replied, referring to a spirit we had just Rescued.

"And I did not believe in many gods. I believed in one, but I never said, and I heard the man call," Aranamus explained, "and that is why I came."

Mary gave us an explanation as to why this spirit from that early a time period was still around. "I've been waiting for her to finish," she said, referring to me. "But I was right here."

"Oh, yes, that was an amazing spirit," said Ruth. "He's been waiting that long?"

"Yes," answered my guide, Mary.

"Then that's about the earliest that has been crossed over by Shirley."

"Yes," replied Mary, "but that was all right because it depends on the quality of the spirit sometimes, and it depends on motives or lack of motives and many different things—"

"This was a very high spirit," Ruth interrupted.

"No. A loving spirit. But it is true that if spirits do not cross over the spirit eventually dissolves or dissipates into the universe. But this one was held in abeyance. His reason for not crossing over had to do with what he experienced."

"Did he fear retribution?"

"No. It's the death of Jesus and the others. He was not a true Roman in the beliefs of their gods, and he was rather confused and concerned as a result."

Mary's explanation helped us to see that there are exceptions to everything including what we have been told by our guides.

CHAPTER II

My Guide, Mary

How does a person get started in this type of occupation? For me it was so simple that I am sure "it was meant to be".

My Uncle Martin had died in 1983, and had not crossed over, so it was getting more and more difficult for my aunt to get over his death, or so it appeared to the family members. I did not know what to do about it, but I did know that I would like to do something. I didn't even know that not all spirits crossed over at the time of death. Frankly, I had never thought about the subject of crossing over. I just assumed that when the body died the spirit left and went to another place. I, myself, had decided that the other place was called the spiritual plane.

My uncle's spirit had hit me on the arm when I tried to use his closet. He had also frightened my sister and seemed to be making his bedroom an uncomfortable place to stay. I had "yelled" at him, but later feeling sorry about what I had done, I decided that the next time I visited his home I would apologize to him. Well, imagine my surprise when I walked into his bedroom to apologize and found a semicircle of spirits waiting for me. That was too much. Something had to be done!

About nineteen months after my uncle's death, I happened to be attending a workshop on mediumship. It was the curiosity factor and not the desire to become a medium that took me there. The medium in charge gave a demonstration of a Rescue. That made me wonder about the fate of my Uncle Martin, because up until then I had never even heard about Rescues. I talked about my uncle and asked if there wasn't something that could be done to help him. The medium in charge used me as the medium to Rescue my uncle. It was so easy that I have been doing Rescues ever since.

Immediately, I was given a spirit guide to assist me in the Rescue work. Her name is Mary and she usually comes through me and speaks to whoever is working with me. It is her job to help me and to help those in spirit who desire to cross over to the spiritual plane. She tries to make sure that everything goes smoothly. I know that she will be here helping with Rescues only as long as I am here on earth because she is my special guide.

Mary has told those who have questioned her that she died when she was sixteen years of age. She also mentioned that she had lived in Cayuga Falls, Ohio. The year she died was 1876. In speaking to her, other people have said that she is very mature for her age. This is Mary's job on the spiritual plane, and in doing this work, she, herself, is growing—spiritually.

One spirit we were Rescuing explained that Mary was "here to open the door and let us (meaning the spirits) through." When my partner asked her if it was "to heaven", she answered it was "to the head", meaning my head. And, of course, the spirit was correct, as I take my spirit out of my body when I become a medium and allow the spirit desiring to be Rescued to enter through the top of my head, through the crown chakra.

My guide, Mary, is like the guardian to the gate. She makes sure that the spirits behave themselves and that they come through in a gentlemanly or ladylike manner. She also seems to help those who are afraid to come through. She definitely doesn't seem to stop those who come to be Rescued hours or days ahead of time, because I feel them. They land on my forehead and cause me to feel a little pressure, perhaps like a small headache. Sometimes, though, it can feel like a large headache and a very persistent one at that!

Here's an example of a spirit who was more interested in letting me know he was ready to cross over than he was in preserving my physical well-being.

"Shirley will be happy because I'm ready to cross over," Monte said.

"When did you come?" Dot asked.

"Just today. I had to let her know I want to come."

"You don't have to bother her."

"But I might not get in if I don't."

"But hitting her on the head won't make you get first in line, will it?"

"It's pretty close to the spot," he replied.

"That's when you jockey for position on her head?"

"At times."

"Is there any sort of system?" Dot wondered.

"Well, last week it wasn't a line...there are a lot here today, but today we are lined up."

There are many times when Mary has difficulty handling the spirits who are waiting to come through me to be Rescued. In fact, from what Mary has said, on different days, I would guess that most of the time she has difficulty.

One day Mary told Ruth, "Yes, I'm having a hard time as you supposedly knew...that's because it's the nature of the spirits who are here today. There can be days when they can all be difficult."

Another day Ruth asked Mary if a ghost we had tried to Rescue had crossed over and Mary replied, "I don't know. I was too busy. When there are spirits waiting to be Rescued, which there are every time, some of them get unruly, and they have to wait their turn. And there's a lot of milling around. Very seldom are they patiently waiting in line...well, there's a lot of other spirits hanging around that don't want to come in, so I have to be really on my toes, so to speak."

Mary even has help. Spirit guides of a higher level introduced themselves and said that they were Mary's helpers. So it's nice to know that Mary doesn't have to do everything by herself when she is helping us with Rescues.

"I come through on the same vibrational wave as the spirits who are earthbound," Mary said. "My vibrational level is changed by the spirit guides here so I can do this." This is a wonderful convenience for me because I, too, can hear what Mary is saying when she speaks to my partner.

When I have a question I wish to ask Mary, I just ask my partner to ask the question, and then Mary will come through me to give the answer. Even that's not necessary as Mary already knows the question because she knows what I am thinking. It's a very convenient arrangement.

When Dot was living and acting as a medium, her guide for doing Rescue work was named Harry. Harry came from Buffalo, New York. I do not remember if Harry told us when he had died, but I do remember him stating that he was forty-six years old.

One time I asked Harry if somebody gave him this job or if he volunteered. "They suggest and you choose from the suggestions the types of work you can do," he replied. "All jobs help people." I inquired as to what other choices they gave him. He smiled. "They're all helping jobs. They're all helping people, so it doesn't matter."

Many spirits have come through singing when it was their turn to be Rescued. An especially popular song is "Zip-A-Dee-Doo-Dah" and I wondered why. Harry said, "Different people sing it. Some of them are so glad to be here. It's a very exuberant, joyous song, so it expresses their feeling."

Mary and Harry are specialized guides. They do not help with the problems of daily living. They help only in Rescue work, and apparently it is only for the benefit of the medium they each work with. Mary told us, "Harry and I are separate. We don't have the same overseer." I'm sure that refers to the higher spirits who help them.

CHAPTER III

Hanging Around

When I talk about Rescues, the question I am asked more often than any other question is, "Why didn't the spirit cross over?" It seems logical to most people that the spirit would just naturally cross over at the time of death, but obviously that is not the case.

Several years before I began to do Rescues, I heard George Gallup speak about a poll, concerning fear, that the Gallup organization had just completed. The number one fear in this country was the fear of death. That was a surprise to me. Since I did not fear death, I didn't think about other people being afraid of dying. But now I think that perhaps that fear of leaving the earth influences a lot of people. Many of them find, what they consider, a very logical reason for hanging around when they find themselves in spirit form.

There are almost as many reasons for not crossing over as there are spirits who have not crossed over. Their thoughts are just as human in death as in life. Their actions and personalities are just the same in death as they were in life. If the spirit was lovable and happy in life, then it will be lovable and happy in death. If it was nasty and ill-tempered in life, then it will be nasty and ill-tempered in death. That is, until the spirit has crossed over and had a chance to change, to grow spiritually.

It seemed to me that this man still had his human personality and his very human emotions. He was still acting as a husband, a human husband. Farmer Sid had decided not to cross over when he died.

"Why did you stay and not cross over?" Dot asked Sid.

"Because another man started seeing my wife right away. I wasn't even buried and he started...he had no business coming. He should have waited a year."

"Did he have a farm?"

"He didn't do good at it...that's why he came running down the road to my house...he was a smart cookie. Well, I didn't like it anyway. I wasn't about to leave!"

When we are doing Rescues, we also ask why the spirit didn't cross over when the body died. Many just want to stay behind to make certain that their families will be all right. Some think that they will be able to exert some influence on those who are left behind. They are just as concerned in death as they were in life. This spirit certainly cared.

"How did you get the blow to your forehead?" I asked H.W., who died in England in 1883.

"Walking the boundary lines, you know," he replied. "Every so often you have to walk."

"Who struck you?"

"They must have been hiding behind the walls. It's a nasty blow."

"Why didn't you cross over?" I queried.

"I loved my land, loved my home, loved Constance—the children."

"Didn't you know you could come back once you had crossed over?"

"They were so distraught. I couldn't leave them."

"Did they know you were there?"

"No," H.W. answered. "They thought I was in the box.!"

This next spirit hung around because he, too, thought he could help his family after he had died. John died in a midwestern city in 1926.

Dot asked, "What happened?"

"I was walking home. Got to the corner—right around the corner—I didn't see it (car) at all. There was a hedge there. In fact, humm, they should have trimmed that hedge. I might not have even looked in that direction. I was thinking about what my sales had been. Our anniversary was coming up, and I was thinking about what to get Minnie," John explained.

"Why didn't you cross over at the funeral?"

"Because Minnie was going to have a lot of trouble. We had a lot of bills. I didn't want to leave her alone."

"And, could you help her?" Dot asked.

"It turned out I couldn't do anything, but I thought I could."

A certain president was asked by Dot why he had not crossed over; why he was still hanging around.

"Tell me, why didn't you cross over at your funeral?"

"Because I honestly thought that I could have some influence on how things—yes, because there were more conferences. Truman still had to go. Harry had to take my place and he would be there with the boys again."

"Were you pleased with the job you did?" Dot asked.

"I was sorry I couldn't finish."

"Were you surprised at how well he managed?"

"No, he was a good man."

"You knew it all along?"

"Yes...I particularly liked his slogan, 'The buck stops here.'"

"That was brave of him, wasn't it?"

"No," he replied, "that was characteristic."

Some spirits don't cross over because their loved ones don't want them to leave. This prevents those left on earth from being able to recover from the loved one's death. They have not said their goodbyes and neither has the deceased said theirs. Jean was one of those who stayed behind because her husband, Larry, wished her to. Athough Jean should have known that it was not the thing to do. It was very interesting to talk to her as she had been a modern English psychic in a city containing a university.

Dot was curious and had to find out why she hadn't crossed over. "Didn't you know that you can see everything just as clearly, if not clearer, from the other side?" Dot asked.

"I was held back by my husband," Jean explained.

"How so?"

"He didn't want me to die and I just couldn't release it."

"Is he still living?"

"Yes."

"How did you die?"

"I was sick for a while. I had cancer," Jean said. "When I died, he knew that I was there and he didn't want me to leave him, and the wish was so strong that I just couldn't make myself leave him."

"Who came for you to take you to the other side?" Dot asked.

"No one came for me, in a way, because when I went to my funeral all my relatives were there—the ones in spirit, that is. They didn't say, 'You have to go with us.' They came, and I said, 'I can't go with you. I cannot go with you. Larry needs me.'"

"There was no attempt at persuasion?"

"No, Larry knew I was there. He could feel me."

"Is he psychic, too?"

"Yes, and he asked me not to leave—not to go—not to cross over."

"If he knew that he might be forcing you to be stuck in a, you know, a long time of darkness, do you think he would have asked that of you?"

"I don't think he knew, and it is 1987, you said?"

"Yes."

"That is not so long."

"No, it's not. You're lucky that you were able to come

through so rapidly. We do get people who have been dead for hundreds of years, however," Dot informed her, feeling that a psychic should know the importance of crossing over at the time of death.

Some spirits are worried about who will inherit their property, their money, their valuables. The sad thing about all of this is they think they can do something about it. But, of course, they cannot.

Hubert, who died in 1855, at age eighty-six, said he was a cobbler, but lived on the family farm. "How many children did you have?" asked Dot.

"I had seven children."

"What was your wife's name?"

"Sally."

"Did she live a good long life, too?"

"No, she died when she had the seventh...I got married again. I married her sister, Sarah."

"Wasn't that handy," Dot said.

"That's not put too well...her sister lived with us anyway. I might as well do something with her."

"How many were living at the farm?"

"Oh, there were a lot of us in the house. My father lived with us, and my brother and his wife, and they had two boys. We all lived in one big farmhouse."

"Well, why didn't you cross over at your funeral?"

"Oh, there were too many problems—too many problems!"

"What were they?"

"What was going to happen to the farm? Would the children be taken care of?"

"Couldn't the others do it?" Dot asked.

"Well, it wasn't that simple 'cause ownership was touchy—and some still lived there...but we all participated in ownership of the house."

Dot asked how it was finally settled.

"I'm not quite sure. I lost track of that...I do not know who owned it after a while."

And that's not unusual. Most of these spirits do not know how things eventually worked out, anyway. After everyone has died or moved away, the spirit may feel lost or confused, and eventually find themselves in a dark void.

Some spirits are afraid that their business will not do as well and they want to make sure that the right person will be taking over the business in their place. Or like this particular gentleman, they wanted to make sure that their customers were happy.

"Now, Sam," I asked, after he had told his story through Dot who was the medium, "what's the last thing you remember?"

"A fire in the shop," he replied.

"That's too bad—and you couldn't get out?"

"I tried to save the suits for the customers. I went back in."

"You came out and then you went back in again?"

"Yes," Sam said. "I wanted to save the suits."

"Did you go to your funeral?" I asked.

"Yes."

"Then why didn't you cross over?"

"I was worried about my customers," Sam explained. "They were going to need their clothes. Who was going to sew for them?"

"So, you hung around, but you couldn't talk to them, could you?"

"Well, I was trying to tell them where to go. I knew who the good tailors were. There weren't many. I was trying to tell them who to see. You can't let people down—you do business all these years—and I did fine work. I didn't want them to go just anywheres, or go to ready-mades. I was a first class tailor. I used to get people coming from all over the country—sent to my shop...you've got to think of yourself as an artist, and you've got to think of the finished product—how it's going to look when it walks out of your store," he explained patiently.

Some spirits have such a low opinion of themselves that they feel they don't deserve to go to heaven. They may be feeling unworthy due to the circumstances of their death. Rosey was one of those whose personal anguish held her back. She was an eighteen year old girl who lived in Ireland three centuries ago.

"I fell through the ice and drowned," she said.

"How did you happen to be on the ice," I questioned.

"I had been sick with a fever and I remember going down to the water."

"Did you have a funeral?"

"Yes—I remember my mother wailing and screaming."

"Why didn't you cross over?"

"I did something stupid and I didn't think I could go to heaven."

Ronald is another example of a spirit who felt foolish or stupid, and therefore, he prevented his own spirit from crossing over. He was attracted to a funeral service I was attending in a Unitarian church (possibly because he had been a Unitarian). He heard me tell someone that I did Rescues, so he followed me home. Ronald said he had lived in the Boston area in the latter part of the nineteenth century.

"They've changed Boston too much. It's not my Boston."

"How did you die?" Dot asked.

"How did I die?" He laughed. "Oh, a train accident."

"Where were you going?" Dot asked, thinking he was on some kind of a trip.

"Oh, I was helping to build—I was laying track. Yes, I was laying track in Boston and I fell off the bridge we were laying the track on. I stepped backward without thinking. I fell to my death."

"Where did this happen? Do you remember the location?"

"Everett. They were carrying dirt and coal..."

"Why didn't you cross over? Didn't they have a nice funeral for you?" Dot queried.

"They had a funeral. My workers came; the people I worked with. And I was in charge, and here I did such a foolish thing! I had some big Polish guys working for me. Oh, did they have muscles. And one man was an American Indian..."

I got Ronald's thought that his family had been well-to-do, but that he had felt ashamed that he worked on the railroad. But, of course, the manner in which he had died was the most painful thought of all, and this prevented him from crossing over.

Violet's reason was rather unusual, but she, too, was feeling unworthy at the time of her death.

"What happened?" I asked her when she came through Dot to be Rescued.

"There was a fire. Danny had been smoking in bed."

"Was he your husband?"

"We weren't married yet, but he kept promising.

"Must have fell asleep. Dropped the cigarette. Then my clothes caught fire."

"How terrible!"

"I died trying to get out of bed. There was smoke and flames. I think he'd been drinking," Violet explained.

"Are you ready to cross over?" I asked.

"We didn't get married, and he promised."

"Why did you stay around so long after the fire?"

"'Cause I wasn't married. He died, too, you know. He didn't even wake up to try and get out of bed!"

"Let's see who comes for you..."

"I see Danny, but how did he get over there?" Violet asked as she began to cry.

"I can't get married over there." Violet resisted crossing over for a while because she was worried that she wasn't married legally.

"I died in sin," she said.

She was finally persuaded to let Danny help her cross over.

For some strange reason we have had very few cases of spirits who were afraid to cross over for fear they would end up in hell, but one I particularly remember is the story of Josiah, who said he was "a man of the cloth."

When Dot asked him how he had died, he told her, "Struck by lightning."

"Did you feel that was a punishment?" she asked.

"I was being punished by God for my blasphemous ways...I had no right to go to heaven!"

"My friend...we're all supposed to go to heaven. God is waiting for all of us...you're not excluded," Dot explained.

"Do you remember your funeral?" she questioned.

"Yes, but I did not deserve to go over. God was punishing me. I was meant to go to hell."

"I think you've been in hell."

"I haven't been to hell yet."

"Did someone you know come from the other side, come to your funeral and beckon you to follow them?"

"Someone was there," Josiah told her, "but they didn't say come with me."

"Who was there?"

"My mother."

"And you didn't go with your mother?"

"No, I knew that I had been struck. I was supposed to go to hell."

When Dot had finally convinced him that he should cross over, his mother came for him and Josiah went with her, but not without some trepidation.

Some spirits are worried that their bodies will not be found, and that is apparently a very important reason for not crossing over. But if the body has not been found, the spirit should still cross over. Their body was the house for their spirit in life, but it is not necessary after death, so hanging around, waiting for the body to be found, will just make it more difficult to cross over later on.

This next example illustrates the case of a confused spirit who apparently felt it necessary that his body be found.

D.R. died in a storm off the coast of Nova Scotia in the mid-nineteenth century. He explained, "I went overboard in a gale— bad northeaster."

"Why didn't you cross over?"

"I was the captain of the ship," he replied.

"And you wanted to stay with your crew," I prompted.

"I wanted to see what happened."

"But you did have a funeral, didn't you? Didn't the ship get back to port?"

"I don't think they found me."

Puzzled, I asked, "And they have to find the body to have a funeral service?"

"I don't know."

"I'm sure your family had a service, though. Did you go spend any time with your family after this happened?"

"I looked in. I could see them, but they couldn't see me."

Another Rescue of a spirit whose body had not been found was that of a Seneca Indian, Wild Water, who died over one hundred years ago.

"How do you live?" I asked.

"I am a good hunter. I bring pelts."

"How did you die?"

"Canoe capsized. I hit my head on a rock...returning from a hunting trip alone."

I was curious. "When you go on a hunting trip, how far away do you go? Does it take several days to get to the area?"

"Depending on season—how I trap and shoot..."

"Why didn't you cross over at the time of your death?" I asked.

"Body not found," Wild Water replied, sadly.

If the person has died a violent death, the spirit is often unable to cross over. It is just too traumatic an experience and many times confusion results. The spirit is just unable to act. The end of life was too much to bear. Don't forget the spirit is still carrying the human personality it had in life, so it is a human reaction it will be experiencing.

We have Rescued quite a few American Indians who were extremely upset because they had been killed, or they had not had the proper burial, or their land had been taken from them. They just wouldn't consider crossing over. It takes a lot of persuading to convince them that they'd be happier in their Happy Hunting Ground.

Acting as the medium, I was aware of a very large Indian of regal bearing. I could also sense that he was very angry. His name was White Cloud.

"Hit on the head with a hatchet," he told Dot. And I, as the medium, felt the whack of the tomahawk on my forehead.

"There was a war," White Cloud explained.

"Was it between Indian tribes?" Dot asked.

"Yes and no. I see Indians and some whites."

"Did you have a proper burial?"

"I do not know what happened after I first died. I just know I am there in the ground. I was killed in a battle."

"Why didn't you ascend to the Happy Hunting Ground?"

"I am protecting my ground (burial ground). It happened many moons ago...before all those intruders came. When there were nice beautiful forests, clear streams, good fishing and hunting...I am protecting my ground—from all those intruders!"

Wind Song was another Indian killed in this fight. He was very sad as he came through Dot, who was now acting as the medium.

"Hurts my heart," he told me. "All those people killed."

"Were you the chief?" I asked.

He nodded his head yes.

"Who killed your people," I asked.

As though still grieving, he replied, "It was Indians with white people. Bad Indians. They had much guns. We no at war..."

"Would you like to go where your loved ones are?"

"My loved ones are all here. Descecrated holy ground. We have many dead buried here: brave warrior, new born infants, respected elders. This is our land and we stay with the land!"

Although we have Rescued many other American Indians, these two were from the same piece of land. This land has a house on it now, and as a result, the Indians felt that the occupants of the house were intruders. The seven Indian spirits we had Rescued from this property had made a pact that they would not cross over as they wanted to guard their burial ground. All the adults in their village had been killed in one terrible attack!

Some spirits don't want to leave because they didn't expect to die. They become hysterical when they realize that they are dead and they are not able to deal with the process of crossing over. This is particularly true of those spirits whose bodies have had a sudden death or an unexpected death like Bebe who was shot by a mugger. She was crying when she came through, and then she yelled, "Oh, hell!"

"What happened to you?" asked Dot.

"I was shot!"

"Do you know who shot you?"

"A mugger shot me. I didn't know I was shot. I was walking in Boston, in Chinatown...in broad daylight. I was going to a Chinese restaurant to meet somebody."

"I don't blame you for crying," Dot said, feeling very sympathetic.

"I'm crying because it shouldn't have happend to me!"

"Well, now you have to get on with other things."

"I don't want to get on with other things," Bebe announced. "I have too much to live for!"

Many young people, especially in their late teens and early twenties, tend to resent the fact that they have died. They feel that they are too young.

Suzanne was meeting a gentleman. "Paul hasn't proposed to me yet, but I'm hoping." The year was 1825.

"What happened?" Dot asked.

"I don't know...I walked out here. This is where we always meet—the gravel path, down from our stable. There's hedges and trees."

"What did you hear?" asked Dot.

"I didn't hear anything."

"What's the last thing you remember?"

"Standing here looking at a tree."

"Do you remember your funeral?"

"Yes!" Suzanne cried. "Paul was there. People were saying, 'Poor Suzanne.'"

"Why didn't you cross over after the funeral?" Dot inquired.

"I didn't want to lose Paul. I'm too young!"

Not too long ago we had a very large group of starving children from Africa who had not crossed over. As we have never had these children before we wondered why we did now. Why were they hanging around? I could see these children as the spirit using my body described them to Ruth. This spirit, named Jesse, saw these children when Ruth asked her to look and see if there were any other spirits who desired to be Rescued. "It's very bright," Jesse said. "Archangels are sending down their light...they look sad. Terrible. They look so small—big heads, big stomachs, skinny bones..."

"How many are there?" Ruth asked.

"Hundreds."

"Tell them to hold hands," Ruth instructed.

"Someone has gotten them together they said...the angels are there. Someone has gotten them together as though the spirit of the gods—I do not know.

"There's seven hundred! I can't even see the end. They're all lying down—oh, bad." Jesse started crying. "And I thought I was bad off."

Ruth took Jesse and the spirits of the children through the Rescue procedure, and as they looked for the light Jesse suddenly cried out. "The light! It's still there. The angels are still with them."

And they all crossed over!

I was quite concerned about so large a number hanging around together and decided to ask Mary, my guide, why this was the case. What an interesting and unusual answer I received.

"This particular group have not crossed over due to the circumstances under which they died," Mary explained. "They thought that they would survive because white people came with food and told them that they would get better. They did not get better and they died, and as a result the anxiety level was too high as they had not expected to die. You might say they were too far beyond help, and they did eat the food. You cannot eat a lot of food. The body will not take it when it has had nothing. And that is what happened to these children. Too much and too late."

There are so many reasons for hanging around the earthly plane, and not crossing over, that it would be impossible to list them all. Suffice it to say, there are as many reasons as there are humans who can think them up. And, being human is what it is all about. The spirit still has the human personality, so it still has the human inclinations.

Knowing that if you don't cross over to the spiritual plane when you die or at your service, that you might wait too long and never be able to cross over, just might be incentive enough for spirits to cross over. I don't think that too many of us wish our spirit to just dissipate into the universe because we have waited too long. And that is what my guide, Mary, said would happen.

Now that there is no longer a body, the spirit should be

willing to go on to the spiritual plane. The spirit should realize that it will not be able to function as it did when it was in a human body. I do not think it is a matter of being stubborn, but rather a matter of not knowing that it can no longer participate in life as it once did.

CHAPTER IV

Suicide

Suicides are so emotionally shaken by what has happened to them that it is extremely difficult for them to cope with anything.

As this particular man came through me he was crying. When he told Dot his name, she recognized the fact that he had been on the news.

"You're going to send me away!" Dennis cried.

"Why?" Dot asked.

"Because I heard what you said before. If you haven't been to your own funeral then you have to go to it." Dennis continued to cry. "I haven't. I just died today! Is it true? I should go first...will I really be better off if I go first...would it be easier?"

Dot could see that he was in complete misery as he continued to cry. She tried to tell him that he hadn't died that day. He was confused about what year it was.

"What happened to my funeral?" he yelled.

"I don't know where to go," he said sadly, and began to cry again. He was in extreme mental pain. "I don't think I should stay!"

"Why did you commit suicide?" Dot asked.

He began crying harder. "I lied to them—lied, lied, lied."

"What happened?"

"I hung myself! It was today!"

Dot asked, "Why did you do it?"

"I didn't love me. I just couldn't take it anymore...all the pressures." And with that he started screaming.

As the medium, my throat was hurting. I could feel the strangling feeling, while the spirit was crying and choking.

"Look for the light," Dot instructed Dennis.

"I'm dying," he insisted.

"You're dead."

As you can see, the emotion is at such a high pitch that it is very difficult to ask questions or reason with the spirit. In a situation such as this it is best to proceed with the Rescue process as quickly as possible.

Dot, as the medium, felt that perhaps this next spirit had not really intended to kill himself. She was sensing his sad feelings as he told his story to me. He was a twenty-two year old college student, who had killed himself more than sixty years ago.

"Call me Randy," the spirit said, in a sad tone of voice.

"Could you tell me something about yourself?" I asked.

"We're wealthy, you know...father is in banking. We have a home in New York City as well as here."

"What happened?"

"I took a gun, and put it in my mouth, and shot myself...because I just couldn't be what Father wanted me to be...everything was fine until it came to my career choice."

"Did you feel good about yourself?"

"Yes, but I just felt I couldn't carry on the family name, the tradition like Dad wanted. I guess I'd been drinking."

"Why didn't you cross over?" I asked.

"I didn't know where to go. I loved it up here, so I stayed here," Randy explained.

"When you had your funeral, didn't anyone come to help you cross over?"

"Well, you see, my friends were so upset. I was feeling terrible at having upset them. I realized I shouldn't have done it and I just wanted to stay and comfort them."

This particular man was very unhappy with his deformities. He believed that he could not go to heaven because of his physical appearance. It was a sad Rescue.

"Hello. Can you tell me your name?" I asked.

"Henry."

"How old are you, Henry?"

"Twenty-seven."

"What's wrong?" I asked.

"I hanged myself," he answered.

"Why?"

"My face was deformed."

"Henry, why didn't you cross over?"

"Heaven is just for beautiful people. There's no place for me to go on to. I'm glad I did it."

"Why?" I wondered.

"I left my body. I didn't like it."

Alice, the lady next door, came for him, and he cried. "She was so good to me," he said.

The spirit in this interview had been dead for almost two months although I had only read about his death nine days before his spirit came to be Rescued. I wasn't surprised when he came, because I had the feeling that he would when I read his sad story.

Donald came through me wailing, "Oooh, oooh."

"Well, who are you?" Dot asked.

"It was hard."

"What was hard?"

"Dying."

"How did you die?"

"I had AIDS. I was sick for a long time and I couldn't take it any longer," he explained in a very weak voice, as he continued to cry.

"And what's your name?"

"Donald Larkin."

"Where did you die?" Dot inquired.

"In my bedroom."

"Were you alone?"

"I killed myself," he told her, still in a very subdued tone of voice.

"How did you do that?"

"With a razor, with a knife. I cut my wrists."

"How old are you, Donald?"

"Fifty-two."

"How did you get AIDS?"

"I don't know if I got it from my partner or where," Donald said. "I'm gay. But he doesn't have it. I don't know where I got it.

"I don't think I really planned it. It just got to be more than I could bear."

"It's over now. Did they have a funeral for you?" Dot asked.

"The church had a beautiful service for me, a memorial service," Donald told her. He seemed to perk up a little at the remembrance.

"It's time to cross over now. Are you ready to go?"

Donald began crying again.

"Donald, it's all over, dear. It's all over. You'll go to heaven now," Dot assured him.

"I don't believe in heaven, anyway." He started to moan.

"Someone that you love is going to come. Tell me when you see the light," Dot quickly instructed.

"There's some light here."

"Anyone you know in that light?"

"No, but I feel at peace. Well, there's some bright light. Well, I don't know who these people are that are here. There's people with me."

"Wait for someone you know," Dot directed.

"I think my grandmother's here," Donald said.

"Is it really your grandmother?"

"Un huh."

"Well, go with your grandmother!" Dot urged him.

"You know," Donald said, "I really pulled the plug on the oxygen."

"Whose oxygen?"

"Mine."

"You mean you didn't cut yourself with a knife?"

"I mean, if I didn't believe in heaven, how can I go to heaven?" he inquired.

"It's just a word. It's where you go after you die. It's where you go when you've completed your chores on earth," Dot explained. "Just go where you were supposed to go in the first place. They've come for you. Go with your grandmother!"

I was told, by Mary, that "all suicides have to come back again because they have not finished the lesson that they have come to earth to perform. Many of them, but not all of them, do not cross over at the time of death. Some do. Some realize that they must," she said.

Sometimes, though, a suicide who really does want to cross over will come to us and ask for help because they are too frightened and traumatized to try crossing on their own.

CHAPTER V

How The Spirits Find Us

Once in a while we ask the spirits how they found us, just out of curiousity rather than necessity. It's interesting to know as there happen to be many different methods of picking up the information about us and our Rescuing.

The spirits might be attracted to a newspaper article I am reading about their death. And many times the spirits have been hanging around in some particular location that I happen to be visiting. They seem to be able to find me very easily, and then they will come home with me.

The spirits might also be attracted to the program I am watching on television. It might be about the area where they had lived. Or, it might be a news program and be about their actual death.

I had been watching the reports of a plane crash on the television for three days. At the same time I had been dealing with several spirits who had arrived on my forehead the moment I first saw the reports of the crash. I asked Ruth to help me Rescue them rather than waiting until our regular day to do Rescues. The first spirit to come through was that of a man who was crying.

"The weather was bad and we told the pilot we thought he should turn around and go back. He said, 'It's a matter of fuel.'

And he was going to try and find a better place to land, and then we hit a mountain or a big hill or something—and then it loomed—there it was. We just couldn't see. It was a mess. It was raining hard. We were like in a low cloud."

"Did anyone survive?" Ruth asked.

"I don't know. I've been here."

"Are there lots of you together?"

"There's some more with me," he replied.

"What's your name?"

"Nat...

"We didn't know this was going to happen...she (meaning me) kept saying to cross over, but we didn't feel good about it. We didn't feel good about it," he explained.

As soon as Nat and his friends crossed over, another passenger came through me to be Rescued.

"It's Ray."

"Were you on the plane?" Ruth asked.

"Yes."

"Nat was here—just a minute ago."

"I know."

"How did you find Shirley? Was she thinking about you?"

"No," Ray replied. "She heard it on the news each day."

Ruth told Ray to stand on her right side and look straight ahead. "Look for the light," she instructed.

"HALLELUJAH!   HALLELUJAH!"

"Do you see someone?" Ruth asked.

"NO! HALLELUJAH!" he shouted. "OH, GOD, WHY DID THIS HAPPEN TO ME?"

Suddenly Ray said, in a very surprised tone of voice, "It's Nat." He crossed over with his friend.

I was very happy when his friend came for him, because I honestly thought that I, myself, might be in a lot of physical turmoil if he didn't cross over soon. My body was feeling the same emotional and physical feelings he was feeling, and they weren't pleasant!

The information that I do Rescues is out on the "air waves", so to speak, and can be picked up by any spirit. All information is known to all spirits except those in human body. Those in spirit are able to find out anything, if they want to find out. Many don't try.

This spirit had been watching television with me.

"Oh, hell!" the spirit said. "I don't know anything. I don't know what I'm doing here. How can I think..."

"Who are you?" Dot asked, as we sat to do Rescues this particular day.

"I don't know. I've been looking at the television and I wonder if it's clouded my thinking. Is that possible?"

"What have you been watching on TV?"

"I've just been watching the news a lot because Shirley's been watching the news a lot...I've been hanging around Shirley...I've waited for you all week—to do this!"

In addition to being an attraction when looking at the news

of someone's death on the television, or when listening to the radio, I evidently attract spirits by the subject matter I may be reading or speaking about. Some spirits come to be Rescued because I have looked at a map or discussed a trip to the area where they once resided when in human body.

My husband and I were planning a trip to Europe and I had been looking at the maps we had in our house. When Frederico, an Italian who lived in London, came to be Rescued, he told Dot how he found us.

"I had observed Shirley, at home, looking at London on a map earlier in the day."

One spirit told us that "a stream of spirits went by" and he followed. Some spirits have said that they were just "carried along in the flow" of spirits and they arrived at the location where we were doing Rescues. One said it was like a long hallway and I could see the "hallway" as he described it.

Dot asked Gregor, "What brought you to us?"

"I don't know. There was, like a stream," he replied.

"A stream?"

"Of spirits," he explained.

"And you just followed the stream? Where were they coming from?"

"I don't know. They were just there."

"Really? And you just fell in the parade?" Dot inquired.

"It's like a stream of movement. It just goes like the wind."

"Really. A current?"

"That is a good word..."

This next account is of a spirit who is in the chapter on ghosts, but I put this part of the conversation he had with Dot here as it is another example of how spirits seem to find us.

Stanley, our friendly sailor, who enjoyed visiting the battles at sea, was asked by Dot how he found us. "Oh, you're well known," he answered.

"We had a friend here a few minutes ago and he was in the Navy in the Pacific."

"That's not how I got here. I've known about you."

Dot was surprised. "Really? For how long?"

"I don't know. A while."

"Have you dropped in on us before?"

"Well, the message is out there. Let's put it that way."

"What's the message?"

"If you want to go."

"Really? If you want to go, do what? Come here?"

"Come where you and Shirley are," he replied. "Wherever you are."

"Is that right?"

"Come any old time."

"Only when we're sitting, please. Don't bother us the rest of the time."

"The air's a little heavier when you're sitting (to do Rescues)...it's like—sometimes things out there are like a vacuum cleaner on a slow motor that's pulling you in," Stanley explained.

"You know how a vacuum cleaner goes 'rrrroom' and if anything's in the way, up it goes. Well, say the motor is a lot weaker, so then—"

This was interesting. Dot couldn't believe what she was hearing. And what made it even more interesting was that she sold vacuum cleaners.

"You get drawn along?" she asked.

"Slower, yeah, yeah."

"And that brings you to us?"

"Yeah. It can. If the energy's in the air it's just like a— some kind of a breeze or an air suction or something. And you just kind of latch on to it."

"Have you gone to other people who have done this?"

"No, I wasn't ready until now."

"Have you heard about other people doing this?"

"No, but I don't know if that means anything. I don't know that much about things. I've just been doing my own thing; I've been a world traveler."

When Howard came through, Dot asked him how he had found us. His explanation was a little different. It sounded as though he had been watching us as we did our Rescues after he found out about us. "I've been observing. I've been around. Word gets around."

After I returned home from a visit to Maine, Sid made it known that he wished to be Rescued. "I just stood around her in Maine," he explained to Dot. "I came to you because it was in the wind. You people are well known, you know."

"Where?" Dot wondered.

"In the spirit world."

"How does word get around?"

"Well, I don't know—osmosis or it's in the wind or—"

This conversation, between Dot and the spirit of an Englishman, occurred about one month before Dot was leaving on a trip. We didn't know if the spirit had just picked the information out of the air, so to speak, or had heard us talking. But it was obvious that he was concerned about all the spirits who wanted to be Rescued. And he also knew about Dot's trip.

"Are there many of you?" Dot asked.

"Yes...many of us. Too many of us. Then we get fearful that nobody will help us. Don't take too long on your trip!"

There have been numerous times when I have unintentionally brought a spirit home with me. They usually sit on my forehead while I am traveling, but sometimes they just come home with me and don't let me know they are with me until we get ready to do Rescues.

While I was cleaning out a closet in a relative's home, I found a pamphlet about a famous radio script writer whose characters I had faithfully followed for years. The script writer came to be Rescued. The first thing Dot heard was a voice singing a radio theme song.

He told Dot, "I haven't been here before, but somehow everything's out there. I wouldn't even have come, but something brought me when Shirley was looking at that old brochure...she's looked at them before, but this one happened to be in her mother-in-law's house..." The information about what I do is out there, and gets picked up by many of the spirits who desire to be Rescued.

Another spirit I brought home with me, who wished to be Rescued, was the artist, Raphael. He found me in the Museum of Fine Arts, in Boston. I was looking at a painting by Van Gogh, and he had read my thoughts about the painting.

When he came through me, neither Dot nor I knew who it was.

"Hello," said a spirit voice.

"Hello," said Dot.

"Hello. Hello," the spirit voice spoke again.

"Who do we have here?" Dot asked.

"Raphael. Raphael," was the answer. "Shirley's been to the Museum of Fine Arts. Ha. Ha. I like to hang around museums. I'm Raphael the painter..."

"Do you remember what year you died?"

"A long time ago—hundred of years. Oh, this is ridiculous! Somebody said, 'In 1492, Columbus crossed the blue.' I think I was in my forties when I died."

"Please, no interference!" Dot said emphatically, addressing the meddling spirits. "Everybody take your turn."

"What got you started in painting?"

"I used to draw in the dirt."

"Who was your first teacher?"

"The master at the chapel," Raphael told her. "Leon, I think was his name. Father Leon. The Duke—he painted for the Duke. It's so hard to remember. It's so long ago. The Duke of Savoy. I had painted beautiful murals on the walls, on his ceilings."

"Are any of those in existence now?" Dot asked.

"I don't know. I do know at one point some idiot didn't like them and painted over some of them! Heresy!" Raphael yelled. "They were religious pictures."

When Dot asked him if he had ever been married, Raphael told her, "When I was young I had a beautiful woman." He began to think about her name. Then he chuckled, "This is strange, because Dulciana comes to me. And Shirley went to the opera yesterday and the heroine's name was Dulciana. I went, too."

"You went with Shirley?" Dot asked in surprise.

"She knew someone was there. She thought it was her father-in-law. She told me to sit between her and the person next to her. That was a good view, and she was right.

"I came home from the museum with her. She and her friend were sketching. Her friend likes those French—oh! They aren't my type at all."

"French painters?" Dot asked.

"Cezanne, Millet. Millet is all right. Oh, and then there was Van Gogh. Shirley was looking at Van Gogh. Oh! I won't say what I'm thinking."

"That's okay," Dot said quickly.

"How did you die?"

"I don't know. It was very painful. I had a pain that got worse and worse and worse. It lasted for several years..."

Changing the subject, Raphael began to expound on museums. "These museums are interesting. They build them differently now. They put lights in the ceilings. They put holes in the ROOF of the building. And they put windows on the roof—even flat roofs! Most interesting!

"Can you see what I'm wearing?" he suddenly asked Dot. It was obvious that he wanted to describe himself.

"No," she answered.

"Well, my pants are quite large. I guess you would call them—they're not like what you are wearing—close to the leg. They are quite billowy, possibly like a sail that is about to be lowered."

"Was there a lot of material gathered?"

"Yes," he hastened on. "And I have a cloak on. My trousers are black."

"What are they made of?" Dot asked.

"Flax," Raphael replied, as he immediately launched into a further description of himself. "And I have a billowy black cloak on. If you wear black the dirt does not show, and you do not have to wash it very often—a white tunic. Humph—I don't know what happened to my legs. They are bare. I should have stockings on. I do not know why."

"Are you lying on a couch?" Dot asked.

"No," he replied. "I'm sitting right here. I've been enjoying Shirley's house, and the opera, and now I am enjoying your house."

When Dot found out that Raphael hadn't had a funeral she wanted to know the reason why.

"I don't know," he said. "I didn't have anything. Seems like there was an uprising of some kind going on—fight. And, like— we were thrown in a common grave!" he told her, shuddering at the thought.

"Do you remember what year it was?"

"You asked me that before," Raphael answered. "Well, I was thinking 1400 something and then that freak said—what did he say—1492, Columbus—well, I don't know who he is."

"He discovered America."

"What's America?"

"It's where you are now, another continent."

"The earth wasn't all there?" Raphael asked in amazement.

"The earth wasn't flat. The earth is round, and he kept sailing west until he bumped into more land," Dot explained.

"The earth is round?" he repeated in disbelief.

"And no one's fallen off? Round," he repeated. "I have never heard that before."

"Are you ready to cross over now?"

"Yes."

"Do you know that I've been to museums in many countries?" he asked Dot. "I enjoy going to them all. I'm so glad Shirley came when I was there."

"She found you in the museum?"

"She didn't know she found me.

"I was here when another Raphael was here (he meant some other time when we were doing Rescues), but then I went and went. Yes, and I did not seem to know how to get back. And she was looking at the old paintings; both (of us) admiring them together, in the same place, at the same time. She was in my period.

"We better get back to what you said. I could be talking too long. There are others here. You see, I didn't know what I wanted to do when I was drawn by the name Raphael before."

He began to tire. "There is a light. It's purple," he told Dot, as his mother came for him.

Needing reassurance, Raphael asked Dot, "Is it going to be all right?"

"Positive, promise you," she replied. "Go and see the masters!"

We were quite excited to have been able to Rescue this famous painter, and Dot's final words were all that he needed.

Sometimes I will be thinking about something and that will attract a spirit who wishes to cross over. A year ago, I was driving home from Maine on December seventh and listening to a program about Pearl Harbor. I knew a spirit landed on my head and accompanied me the rest of the way home. I had his company for about an hour of travel time.

That afternoon Dot and I sat to do Rescues and this spirit came through. "What stimulated you to come at this time?" Dot asked.

"Well," the spirit replied, "it has been on these machines, these boxes called TV. That is only one reason...well, I felt it wasn't necessary to stay on this level anymore, but the biggest reason of all you haven't even recognized. What is today's date?"

"Today is the day that the Japanese bombed Pearl Harbor."

"That is correct...Shirley was listening to the car radio, the news, all the way home from Maine. And she was thinking about Pearl Harbor and glad that she wasn't going to Hawaii today, because she felt that her trip would be ruined, that she would have so many spirits on her head."

He was correct. I was thinking about Pearl Harbor. I was planning to go to Hawaii in a few months and was worried that when I went to the Pearl Harbor Memorial I would be inundated with the spirits of those who had died there.

After he crossed over, Dot asked me if I knew who it was. I knew. I could see the glasses with a little wire rim and the things were sitting right on my nose. "I could almost feel the little thing sitting right on my nose!" I answered emphatically. So he did identify himself without using his name. And, of course, we both knew it was President Roosevelt!

Traveling to other parts of the world can also attract spirits, although we don't really have to leave town in order for spirits from other countries to find us.

When Dot came back from Germany, Amelia, who was from Munich, Germany, came to be Rescued. She told me, "I knew you were doing this...I've been traveling a lot. Dorothy was in Germany. Dorothy was in Munich. Dorothy was thinking about Munich this weekend. She was seeing the mall and the store...my father had the store."

Then we proceeded to have one German after another every time Dot mentioned she had been to Germany, or even when she mentioned that she'd like to go back.

We don't have to know their language, if it is foreign, and they don't have to know ours. If we are thinking and a spirit picks up our thoughts, there is no language barrier because thoughts are not in language. And if the spirit comes through the medium, the spirit uses the medium's mind, and again there is no language problem.

Hearing a name similar to their own will draw a spirit's attention. We had this visitor almost a year after I came back from England. Marian may have been attracted to us at the time she came because we had just finished Rescuing a woman with an almost identical name. Dot acted as the interviewer.

"Good afternoon," the spirit said.

"Good afternoon," Dot replied. "And what is your name?"

"Well, my name is similar to Marianne and you were talking to a Marianne, and I came."

She told Dot that she had been in the Ashmolean Museum in Oxford. She meant in spirit form. "Shirley was there last year...I saw her there."

Astonished, Dot asked, "You saw her there? How could

you pick out Shirley from all those people that pass through?"

"That was easy."

"Why?"

"Because she has a different kind of energy field."

"Because she's a psychic?"

"Yes."

That made me feel like some kind of a magnet.

I happen to enjoy mysteries and always try to watch *Mystery* on Public Television. I had been watching a program about a police inspector in the city of Oxford, England, one Sunday night.

When Philip came through to be Rescued the next day, he told Ruth, my new partner, "I came because Shirley was watching the Inspector Morse mystery on TV."

"Were you a don?" Ruth asked, as she too had been watching the same program.

"No. Well, what interested me is that this is about murder in the church and I was a vestryman...and I was not too happy. Not too happy."

"Why not?"

"Not too happy to desecrate the church with all those murders!"

"It was very high church," Ruth started to say, but was unable to finish.

Philip interrupted her to say, "It was the proper religion."

Some spirits are attracted to us because they hear us discuss an event such as a plane or train crash and they have died in a similar accident. Sometimes it is the same crash we are talking about. Other times we will be discussing some other news event. It doesn't matter what it is, if someone has died in it they will quite often be attracted to us.

You might say that our bigggest event each year is in March as we approach St. Patrick's Day. Usually the week it falls in, and the preceding week, are filled with spirits from Ireland, and Irish men and women in this country. It's as though they wait for this particular time of the year. However, I really think it's because the holiday attracts them and that they wouldn't have come otherwise. We Rescue the Irish all during the year, but not like we do each March. They come through one right after the other, and there would be no end to them if we did not stop when we felt we had to.

Here's a sample of the spirits we had in the middle of March one year.

"You're getting the Irish today. There's an English girl in there," Patrick said, referring to the spirits who were waiting to be crossed over. "It's not her day!"

The next one to come through said, "Well, you wouldn't believe it, but it's another Irish person. Notice I didn't say Irishman. My name is not and will never be a man's name," so spoke Mary, who took in "other people's washing."

"Happy St. Patrick's Day to you, too," the next spirit said. "Can't say 'top of the morning' 'cause it's afternoon."

John Francis was the next Irishman. "It's way back in the days of glory, and the Irish are beginning to come and come and come," he told Dot. "I was from Boston...I was born right on the button—1800...my birthday is in March. Guess what day?" And, of course it was St. Patrick's Day.

Some people ask me to find out if a certain person has crossed over, not because the spirit is annoying them, but because they will feel better when they know that they have. So when we are sitting to do Rescues we will ask for that person. But we don't necessarily have to ask for them as they know their loved ones are concerned, and they will come and tell me they have crossed over. If they haven't crossed over, they will come when I inquire about them and willingly be Rescued. They have simply picked up this information from the air waves, you might say.

I wouldn't be surprised to learn that the reason we have so many spirits from England has to do with the fact that I lived in England in my last life and am very interested in that country.

Since Mary, my guide, came from Ohio, a great majority of our American spirits, needing to be Rescued, are from Ohio. They seem to be attracted to Mary. So you see, there are all kinds of reasons for the spirits to be attracted to us.

When Ruth, my new partner, began working with me, she didn't really understand how the many different spirits could find us, no matter where we were. So Mary tried to explain it to her.

"It's hard to explain this to you and I've tried to explain it to Shirley and Dot also," Mary said. "Some spirits say they come on a stream of air. Some spirits say they're in layers. In other words, they were saying all different things, but it is because it is not quite the same thing for each of them. But when they are coming it is not the same thing as when they are here.

"There are different energy waves, so the spirits do not even perceive them the same way. Each energy wave is its own energy wave and its characteristics are totally different than each of the others.

"Each spirit has its own reality, as do you, and Shirley, and everyone else."

"It's almost poetic," Ruth said.

Mary laughed. "Well, she doesn't think it's poetic," she replied, referring to me. Mary knew I didn't like the spirits landing on my forehead to let me know that they were waiting to be Rescued.

"And I did explain to you before, why it doesn't feel as strong as it did before when Dot was alive."

"Could you tell me again, please."

"Because Dot was also a medium, and the energy was stronger and of a different type than it is with you...the energy is different and the waves are different, naturally, as they are for each person. But the level is different when you are a medium.

"And when they (the spirits) are here I try to layer them...if you can picture a layer cake."

"Why?" Ruth inquired.

"Because there are times, if I do not do this before you

begin, then there is a big jumble all around the two of you—"

"And it is very hard to get in," Ruth guessed.

"Yes. So, I try to layer them, but it is not—the closest I can explain it is the layer cake..."

I don't know if Mary's explanation of how the spirits find us and how she must organize them makes things clearer or more confusing.

Being told that the spirits find us by following a stream of air might really mean they are following a stream of energy that might be put out by us. The energy that is emitted by me, and by the television set, seems to be enough or of the right kind to attract spirits. Our thoughts are energy. Our voices are energy. The television is energy.

I think the conclusion to all of this can be deduced from what I have presented in this chapter. It's obvious that all information is available to those in spirit, and can be picked up and used by them if they so desire. That information is in the form of energy.

Mary has stated that Ruth and I have energy waves which are of a different nature than those of Dot and me when we worked together. But even though they are not as strong, apparently that fact does not prevent those spirits who are stuck on the earthly plane from being able to find us so that they might be Rescued.

CHAPTER VI

Quite A Variety

The variety of spirits we have Rescued is infinite. We have Rescued the rich and the poor and those in-between. We have Rescued adults and children. There have been spirits of famous people and spirits of infamous people. It makes no difference to us who it is. If we can help the spirit to cross over, we do so. They seem to know that, and as a result, we have had the spirits of famous people such as presidents, prime ministers, mayors, writers, actors, singers, artists, playwrights, and astronauts.

We have Rescued members of the animal kingdom. They also have spirits and need to cross over to their spiritual plane.

We have also Rescued the spirits of criminals such as murderers, gangsters, spies, bootleggers, and thieves. Death does not seem to have changed the attitude of the criminals. There is no remorse for whatever crime they have committed, whatever harm they have done to others. There is no repentance because of death. I can only speak for them when they are in the earth-bound state. We don't make any judgments as far as the spirits are concerned though, as we are just helping them to cross over.

This murderer had no remorse. He was just doing his job. "My name is Lenny Springer. You don't know me. I'm a hit man."

"Who do you work for?" Dot asked.

"Nobody big...I get contracts. I work on my own mostly. I'm not going to squeal," he protested.

"You don't have to be afraid," Dot assured him. "They're all dead now."

"The big guys? They're all dead? So—so am I," he snickered.

"Why didn't you cross over when you had your funeral?" she asked.

"Didn't wanna go. Too much excitement...oh, I made a lot of payoffs. People that didn't cooperate."

"Did you enjoy doing that?"

"It's a way of earning a living," he said, sounding defensive.

"It didn't bother you to have people die?"

"They were just as bad as me. They were doing something illegal, too...a lot of bootlegging going on. That was where I mostly had my business..."

"And you thought you were a big shot because you had so much more money?" teased Dot.

"No, I didn't think I was a big shot...I was good at what I did. I was good at planning. Gotta plan these things. Don't just walk in."

Lenny made his killings sound so business-like.

One time we had a very strange situation when the victim of the murderer came to be Rescued, and the murderer came through immediately after we finished. The victim was the wife and the murderer was the husband. I was acting as the medium.

The spirit was crying and seemed very sad. "It's so cold," she gasped.

"Tell me your name so I can help you," Dot said. "I must have your name."

"Gloria Gordon," the spirit whispered.

"Why is it so cold, Gloria? Are you in the water?"

Gloria nodded.

"How did you get in the water?"

"I was thrown," she answered in a whisper.

"You were thrown? Who threw you into the water?"

"My husband."

Dot was astonished. "Your husband! Why would he do that?"

"He strangled me."

Gloria was so cold she was shivering, which meant that I was cold and shivering. "Oh, it's cold..."

"And what made your husband do such a terrible thing to you?"

"My husband loves somebody else, a younger woman...he was younger than I am...he didn't kill me all the way before he threw me in the water..."

Suddenly Gloria became hysterical. She let out a great cry of anguish, "My husband is here!"

"Is he sorry for what he did?" Dot asked.

"I don't know," Gloria cried. "I want to get out of here!"

At this point she saw a light and crossed over as fast as she could.

Immediately I could feel the presence of another spirit.

"Hello," a deep voice greeted Dot.

"Hello there," she answered. "What's your name?"

"Clifford."

"Clifford what?"

"You know," was the response.

"Gordon?"

"Gordon," he confirmed.

"What's the last thing you remember?"

"Dying of old age."

"With your lady love?"

"No, she left me...she left me when I killed my wife."

"That was a terrible thing to do!"

"I hate my wife," he replied in a very calm voice.

"You still hate her?"

"She didn't respect me!"

"Well, she's gone over and she's with people who respect her.

"Look for the light," Dot instructed Clifford.

"Nothing turned out to be good," Clifford stated flatly, as he saw the light and crossed over.

There certainly wasn't any remorse there.

I can remember only one crime in which the perpetrator was sorry for what he had done. A young man had been caught stealing a horse and was shot.

"It was a very bad number," Patrick told Dot. "I was in a fight with a farmer. I took more than his horse. I'm sorry now. I wasn't then. I think I was a nasty sort of person. I was drinking too much. I would be mean at times."

Most of the time it is just ordinary people who want to be crossed over, but many of them have very interesting stories and we always enjoy talking to them.

If the spirits tell us names, dates, and places of a historical nature we look this information up in our own encyclopedias to corroborate their stories. I can attest to the fact that not all spirits can accurately remember all facts. One example was when a friend's father couldn't remember his wife's name even though the friend knew she was speaking to her father. We, here on earth, are known to forget facts at times, and many of us have difficulty remembering names!

We also have a category we call the "Hollywood types" as we're not sure who they really are. We think they were movie stars when alive, but they tend to give incorrect or distorted information as though they don't really care to identify themselves. If they aren't willing to give us their true names, first and last, then we ask them to leave and not come back until they are ready to behave. Most of the time they don't come back.

We have had spirits who tried to make us think they were Clark Gable, Basil Rathbone, and Leslie Howard among others. After researching them in our public library, I would prefer to think that they might have been who they hinted they were.

However, since much of their information did not prove to be accurate when researched, we just put them in our "Hollywood types" category—name unknown.

We have Rescued all different ages with the exception of babies and very young children under the age of five. I was told by Mary's spirit guides that the old soul theory applies to them. They don't come to be crossed over because they all do cross over at the time of their death. It seems their memory is so fresh that they simply cross over immediately at the time of their death. The one exception to this is the fact that we have Rescued quite a few women who were carrying their babies with them. Apparently they died in childbirth along with the infant.

There have been young children, though, at the age of five and older who often have unusually sad stories.

"My name is Cindy," said a little voice. "You wanna know who I am? You're not gonna be upset? I'm a Brownie."

"Oh, welcome. Welcome, Brownie Cindy," answered Dot. "I didn't know we had Brownies in America."

"Ha, ha, ha, ha! I'm a Brownie, a Girl Scout Brownie! You thought I was a little Brownie. Well, I'm about three feet tall, but I'm not that kind of a Brownie."

"How old are you?" Dot asked.

"I'm seven and a half," Cindy answered.

"Tell me, what's the last thing you remember?"

"I think it's the school playground."

"Did you fall off the swing?"

"I think I fell and hit my head. I don't feel the bump now... I was climbing up—ooh, I was climbing up on the fence—we're not supposed to do that—and I fell and hit my head. They had, like, white stones. The swings were set in white stone. There was a swing near the fence. I fell back off the fence and hit my head. I was up the fence pretty high because my feet just fit in those holes."

"Do you remember having a funeral?" Dot asked.

"I didn't want to leave my Mommy and Daddy," Cindy explained as she began to cry.

"Did they have any other children?"

"They had my little brother after I left them."

"What brought you to us?"

"I don't know. I just heard St. Patrick's day."

"And what does that mean to you?" Dot asked.

"That's my birthday."

This little girl came through me crying. I had heard about her death when I was on a vacation trip. "I want my Mommy and Daddy," she told Dot.

"You want your Mommy and Daddy?"

"I left them."

"How old are you?"

"Five."

"What happened?" Dot asked.

"My apple rolled under the bus...I wanted to get my apple for lunch, and I crawled under the bus to get it," Nancy explained.

"Where was the bus going?"

"To school."

"Oh, honey, I'm sorry. Everybody was very, very upset to hear about that," Dot told her. Dot was also very upset.

"It's your turn to go to heaven. Are you ready to cross over, honey, into the light?"

"I don't know about heaven...I don't want to leave my family."

Teens, young adults, middle age, old age, but not a disproportionate number of elderly—these are the spirits of people, at any and every age, who do not want to leave the earthly plane and cross over to the spiritual plane after they die. And they all have their reasons.

And, now of course, we are also Rescuing animals. The animals usually appear with their masters or mistresses, but sometimes there are groups of animals who died in a common disaster. There have also been wild birds and wild animals.

Joining hands doesn't always apply though. One day there was a group of dogs in line waiting to be Rescued. This was a surprise to me because it was only the second time that we had ever encountered animals desiring to be Rescued. I could see several different breeds of dogs, all large in size. There were German shepherds, chows, and large white dogs with long fur who had black and brown spots in the shoulder area.

John, the spirit of a seventeen year old boy, who had died in an automobile accident in Maine, came through me to be Rescued.

He also described the dogs. He said that they had died in a kennel fire. Ernie, who was my partner then, didn't know how she was going to be able to cross them over because she didn't know how they could possibly hold hands. The process turned out to be very successful. We were instructed to have them hold tails and it worked. They all crossed over together!

An interesting Rescue, involving an animal, was that of a zoo keeper and his giraffe. Benny was the spirit of the man who came through to be Rescued.

When Benny had completed the description of his life, Ernie, who was doing the interviewing, asked him, "So is there anyone else around who wants to go with you?"

"Oh, I don't know. I haven't been paying attention. Oh, this young lady here nudged me. Yes. Her name's Mary." (That was my guide.)

"All right, Mary. Tell everyone to hold hands."

"Oh, she says I have to tell you who's here."

"Okay, let's hear."

"Oh, oh, first one—this is funny. The first one—this man's with a giraffe!"

"Holy mackeral!" Ernie exclaimed under her breath.

"He was a zoo keeper," Benny laughed. "And he brought his giraffe with him? Ha, ha, ha."

"I don't blame him. That's nice."

"His name is Manny," he said, still laughing.

"Okay. Manny and his giraffe," Ernie said.

"Manny and his giraffe," Benny repeated. "He says Chicago Brookfield Zoo."

"Chicago Brookfield Zoo."

"Yes, yes, he was an animal keeper. He took care of the giraffe and the elephants and the rhinoceros."

"All right," Ernie said, "let's cross the giraffe over as well."

Since this episode with Manny and his giraffe, we've Rescued many other kinds of animals such as an elephant, lion, sheep, dogs, horses, and even cows who let it be known they were upset because they had been shot.

I have been told by one of Mary's spirit helpers that the animals go naturally, though obviously that is not true all of the time. And although they are of a different dimension, if they so desire to be with their masters there is no problem. Therefore, there is no problem with them coming to welcome their masters when the spirits of their masters are ready to cross over. Birds, too, are of another dimension.

One of the biggest surprises Dot and I ever had was the November day that we Rescued our one and only leprechaun. I didn't believe in leprechauns before that day, but I certainly did afterwards.

"I still see the rainbow," said the child-like voice of the spirit who was using my body.

"Who are you?" Dot asked.

"I'm a little leprechaun," came the reply.

"And where do you come from?"

"Ireland."

"Do you have a name?"

"Sammy."

"How old are you, Sammy?"

"Thirty-two."

"Why do you say you're a leprechaun?"

"I AM a leprechaun!" he announced.

"You're the first one we've had," Dot explained. "Tell me something about yourself."

"You can't see me?" he asked.

"No."

"Oh! How sad," Sammy said. "Can you tell I have a pointed nose?"

"Yes." Dot had become aware of his nose as he spoke. "Shirley can feel it," she continued, as I touched my nose and indicated my awareness of its new shape.

"What are you wearing?" Dot inquired.

"What do leprechauns wear?" he demanded.

"I don't know. Little pointy hats and pointed-toed shoes, curled up—"

Sammy interrupted with a giggle. "Pointy!" he said.

"That's true, is it?" pressed Dot.

"Yes, it is."

"You're about three and a half feet tall?"

"I don't think I'm that big."

"Project a very good picture of yourself to Shirley so she

can describe you to me later," Dot directed him. "What colors are you wearing?"

"Now what colors do leprechauns wear?" he demanded.

"Red and green," replied Dot, remembering a little Christmas Elf doll about seventeen inches tall that she had, for some reason, been recently picturing up on a shelf in its accustomed holiday spot in her living room.

"Red!" he snorted.

"Sorry about that," Dot apologized.

"Green! The Emerald Isle!" corrected the leprechaun.

"Yes, green," she agreed.

"Red! Where did you get red?" he demanded to know.

"I was thinking of a little trim. Maybe I'm thinking of a Christmas Elf. Just green?"

"Just green."

"Okay. Well, this is quite interesting—that we're having a leprechaun come through. Tell me something about yourself."

"Most people know about leprechauns," he retorted.

"What part of Ireland are you from?"

"I am from Derry," he answered with a giggle.

"Are leprechauns born the same way humans are born?" Dot asked.

But before Sammy could answer, he was startled by a sudden noise across the room.

"It's just the door creaking," assured Dot. "It's nothing but the wind."

"Do you have ghosts?" he asked anxiously.

"Oh, yes, from time to time," she answered nonchalantly.

"Is there something behind the door?" he whispered, fearfully.

"My husband is in there eating his lunch, that's all."

"Is he safe?"

"Oh, yes. You're safe," Dot reassured him, as Sammy seemed seriously concerned for his safety. "What do you know about ghosts?" she asked.

"They make me a little nervous."

"Because why?"

"Hm. Just have that—little feeling."

"Can you see them? Are you always able to see them?"

"Well, I see them," he replied.

"How do you protect yourself against ghosts and other things?"

"I don't have to protect myself."

"You don't? And what is your function? What do lepre-chauns do?"

"I bring happiness."

"Is that right? How do you do that?" Dot wondered.

"Oh, I do little things for people...I make things happen," he replied cockily.

"Is that right? What year is it?"

"The year 1721, comes to me, but I don't really know because I don't really care. I could be wrong."

"That's all right.   Are leprechauns an ongoing phenomenon?"

"Oh, there are always leprechauns in Ireland," Sammy informed her.

"Do they stay in Ireland?"

"Well, I don't know. I mean, the ones I know do."

"Can you wish for a leprechaun to come?"

"Why? Are you Irish?"

"No, not this time. I might have been in another lifetime."

"Well, I don't know that answer. I, uh, this is not Ireland!" he said, getting slightly upset at Dot's suggestion.

"Is it in England that they have Brownies, which is something like leprechauns?"

"Oh, they are like a cousin, in a way. Not a factual cousin, but something like us, only they go into the houses. Well, we don't go into the houses.   They do things in the houses— housework, but we are more like, oh, you find a gold piece when you need it the most. Or, you find a sweetheart when you need her the most. Or, someone comes along and gives you a ride just at the right time."

"Oh, I have one of those!" Dot exclaimed.

"One of those? You have a leprechaun?" Sammy asked in wonderment.

"I appear to have a force that helps me when I need it," she explained.

"A leprechaun?" he persisted.

"I don't know if it's a leprechaun, but I have some guiding force that helps me in difficult situations. For instance, if I get a flat tire—"

"Flat tire? What is that?"

"Oh, some sort of disablement to a moving vehicle."

"You speak in a strange tongue," said Sammy.

Dot tried again. "If a wheel fell off my wagon, okay?"

"I have a feeling you don't have a wagon," he chided.

"No. I have something that moves along without a horse. It's called a motor. If something happened, it would happen at a place where either I could drive right into a facility where they fix those things, or somebody would come along and stop for me immediately," she explained. "I've always had good fortune or found money when I needed it."

"You don't need a leprechaun then."

"Do you know how you died?"

"No," he replied in a sad whisper.

"Is it strange that you didn't go over to Leprechaun Heaven after you died?"

"Wait! Wait! I'm trying to think. You asked me a question. I think I was in a battle or a fight—some evil force. But I don't remember what it was. It's like I can see something that's black and brown and all flying around," he replied with extreme agitation. "But I can't identify it."

"That's all right," soothed Dot. "Give me your whole name," she said, changing the subject in an effort to calm him.

"Samamusoto, but everybody calls me Sammy," he said brightly. "That was my whole name. One name."

"Does it have a meaning?"

"Well, what came to me was Little One of the Elf Kingdom."

"That sounds lovely. Now let's see if we can spell it."

"Spell it? What's that?"

Dot tried to pronounce his name. "Did I say it correctly?"

"Oooh! It sounds terrible when you say it."

"Please say it again. I want to get it right."

"What you call the spelling—there isn't any, so how can you—? Just call me Sammy."

"All right, Sammy. Do you have any brothers or sisters?"

"It doesn't work that way."

"Where did you come from?"

"Energy. A driving force."

"That's beautiful," said Dot, as she thought about it.

"Something stomped me out," he explained, with intense emotion. "This big brown and black thing! It was evil!"

"And you don't know why you didn't cross over into Leprechaun Heaven? What kept you around? Did you feel that you hadn't completed your assigned tasks?"

"I don't think that it was meant to happen. I don't know what—why it happened. I didn't think anything like that was supposed to happen to a leprechaun."

"How long do leprechauns usually live? Do you have any

idea?"

"Usually live? That means how long we are there?" he asked, trying to understand the question Dot had asked him.

"Yes."

"Oh, centuries."

"Oh, then you died as a mere child, in time.

"All right. Well, I suppose since you are here I'm supposed to send you along the way I do everybody else," Dot decided. "Are you ready to cross over into the light?" she asked.

"If that's what I am supposed to do. You can't send me back to Ireland?" he asked hopefully.

"I'll try. Do you want me to try that first?"

"Well, I don't know what I'm supposed to do."

Neither did Dot.

"Why don't we ask the Supreme Creator to send you where you're supposed to go, and we will use our usual methods." Dot paused. "Sammy?"

He was suddenly gone, and I, who had been the medium through whom he had manifested, explained.

"Do you know what happened?" I asked Dot. "A rainbow appeared and he went with the rainbow. I don't know where he went...he went on the rainbow!"

"He saw the rainbow from the beginning," Dot reminded me.

"But he didn't see it again," I replied. "He said, 'A rainbow is here.' But—"

"But he didn't know what to do," Dot interrupted. "You gave him a ride on a rainbow!"

"That's interesting—and weird," I said, laughing. "I'll bet you didn't know what to do."

"I was stalling," she admitted.

I was in gales of laughter now, picturing Dot trying to figure out how to cross over a leprechaun.

"Waiting for inspiration. Waiting for orders," she explained.

When Dot asked Sammy to project a picture of himself, I could see him standing next to my chair, the top of his hat level with the top of the chair cushion. When we measured the height later that day, it was exactly the same height as Dot's Christmas Elf doll, seventeen inches!

I could see his green pointed cap and the green pointed shoes, but I didn't see one bit of red on him. I knew he was highly insulted at that suggestion. He had on a very plain outfit, but he was completely in green.

"When you asked him what part of Ireland he was from, I pictured a rock, and the rock was larger than he was," I told Dot. "But the rock was smooth, so it must have been very old. The rock was above him, but it went down at an angle, and it hung over on one side. That must have been his home...because when you asked him where he was from in Ireland, that's the first thing he saw," I explained.

Approximately one year later, when Dot and I were

listening to the tape recording of this event, Sammy came through me for a brief moment and said, "Thank you, Dot." What better reward could we have received!

CHAPTER VII

The Continuing Experience

Not all spirits realize that the body is dead, and the spirit using my body, thus using my mind and my voice, may speak in the present tense. We call this a "continuing experience" because the spirit thinks that it is living the dying experience, and it continues to live it year after year after year. In fact, the dying experience does not end for these spirits until they have been Rescued. Of course, once they have crossed to the other side these spirits know that they have died. The only problem is they have to be convinced that they have died in order for us to persuade them to cross over to the spiritual plane. This can be very difficult, and it sometimes takes an extremely good sales pitch to make them believe that they have really died.

When spirits having a continuing experience come through my body, my body assumes the position of their body at the time of death. If they are lying on their death bed, then I feel like I am lying on a bed. If pillows were propping them up, then I feel like pillows are propping me up. If they died of a heart attack while running up a hill, and are out of breath, then I have chest pains and am feeling out of breath. In other words, I feel the same physical symptoms they feel when they are in me, as these spirits are continuing to live out the experience of dying.

"Oh, my throat!" Derrick complained as he came through me. "Oh, it feels so dry!" Then he yawned. "I'm so tired, too. Oh, I'd just like to go to sleep...oh, I need a tissue. Oh, I need to blow my nose. Oh, I'm filling up. Oh! Get me a tissue," he instructed Dot. "Oh, it's filling up awful."

My nose began filling up and I felt like I really did need a tissue. I felt like my nose needed blowing.

Rosalie was having a continuing experience as she came through me one day when we were doing Rescues. My body began to feel tired, and I began to slump in my chair. I was really tired. I felt like I just wanted to go to sleep.

"It's hard," Rosalie said. "I can't sit up." Neither could I.

"Where are you?" Dot asked, when she saw my body sliding down in the chair. "In your bed at home?"

"No. I hate this place," Rosalie responded tearfully.

"Where are you?"

"In a nursing home. They put me here and they won't let me out!" Now she really began to sob. "It's hard to sit up."

Rosalie told Dot she was eighty-two and lived in Hollywood, California. She and Dot then talked about different things that had happened in her life.

Dot knew she had to force the issue. "Rosalie, did you know that you're dead?"

There was a pause and then a terrible scream. "Oh! No! No! No! .I'm not dead! You're just saying that!" It was obvious that she did not know that she had died, nor did she want to believe it.

"It doesn't feel any different dead or alive. Your spirit didn't go anywhere. You just think you're still in the nursing home," Dot said, trying to assure her. "You can let go of the body now. What are you afraid of?"

Rosalie was sobbing so hard she had difficulty answering. "I want to get out of here."

"Well, you are out."

"Not that way!"

"You don't need the body anymore. The body wore out and you moved on."

"A brand new body?" she asked.

"Yes," Dot replied. "You've got to go on."

"A brand new body?" she repeated, incredulously. "How do you get a brand new body?"

"You've got to go to heaven first. You've got to let go of the earth and this old worn out body and all these thoughts and go on...that's just the empty body. It's like a house that wore out, crumbled and fell to the ground. You've got a whole eternity ahead of you—of life, of living, of designing, or doing whatever you want."

Rosalie didn't even know if she had been given a funeral, but Dot was able to convince her that she would be happy again if she crossed over.

I always seem to feel tired when a spirit enters who is having a continuing experience. My body became extremely tired when this spirit came through, and I could hardly stay awake.

"What's the last thing you remember?" Dot asked Jerry, who was a Hollywood stuntman.

"I was walking on the edge of a building...and I fell."

"What was the movie?"

"The movie was with Douglas Fairbanks or somebody..."

"And there wasn't any protective netting?"

"When I fell—there was a gust of wind—and it caught me off balance," he explained. "Oh—I hit a tree—and then it got me."

"This was not on the set?" Dot inquired.

"No, we were filming downtown. And I didn't die yet, but I know I'm gonna die 'cause they got me so under I can't even keep my eyelids open," Jerry replied.

These spirits sincerely believe that they are still in the environment they were in when they died. Not knowing they have died, they insist they are in their bedrooms, or the hospital, or wherever they were when they did die. And they see their surroundings as they were.

"I'm in my bedroom! I can see my wallpaper!" Frederick insisted when Dot tried to tell him he was in her living room.

Since the spirit is still reliving the death experience, everything that did occur at the time of death is still occurring, and seems very vivid as far as the spirit is concerned. This spirit thought he was still on the Erie Canal.

"Hello," said Dot. "Who are you?"

"I'm a canal boat captain. Been doing this sixteen years.

"Oh, there's a barge problem!   There's going to be an accident and I can't stop it!"

"What's happening?" Dot asked.

"The boat is crashing into lots of barges!"

When the spirit can see what is happening, then I, too, can see the same thing as the spirit is seeing through my eyes.   This spirit thought he was still seeing the streets of London.

"Well, I can see the shops and I can see the cobblestone street.   I can't see anything happening," he told Dot.

"The street I'm on I'm not familiar with...I don't recognize this street.   I must have been on an errand of some sort."

"Is it night?" Dot asked.

"It's broad daylight.   I can see everything."

The spirits actually believe that the person interviewing them is the interloper.   That's why Samuel was annoyed with Dot.

"I'm congested," Samuel explained as he coughed.

"You left the body and you're dead and buried," Dot replied.

"My body's right here!"

"No, that's Shirley's body."

"I can feel it," he said, as he tapped my chest thinking it was his.

Dot tried to convince him that he had died and would be better off if he crossed over, but Samuel would have none of it. "I've had it with talking to people.   I want peace and quiet."

"What kept you here?" Dot inquired.

"Oh, this sounds so petty. I really am dead? Well, why am I sick in bed? Oh, my chest." He began coughing again.

"I'm really annoyed," he said. "You're really very, very nosy—just a gossip."

"You came to my house," Dot replied.

"I did not come to your house! You're in my bedroom. Well, I'm in my bedroom. I don't know where Lydia is, but I'm in my bedroom. For shame, talking that way."

There are times when the Rescue seems especially realistic, and not only am I able to see what the spirit sees, but I feel as though I am actually there. Although this is consistently true with a continuing experience, some experiences make a stronger impression upon me than others.

I had been on a trip to northern California two months earlier, and as a tourist had journeyed to the Muir Woods. In this experience with Amy I felt like I was there again!

"I'm dying," the spirit said.

"What's your name?" Dot asked.

"Amy. I'm in a forest on a California mountain...I'm alone. I can't get down. I'm too weak."

"How did you get there?"

"I went with a group of people. We were mountain climbing...we had a storm—a flash flood—and we all ran for cover out of the way of the rushing water and I got separated from everybody else.

"I don't have anything to eat or drink."

"How many days have you been alone?"

"I don't know. I passed out a few times. I know it was sunny. It rained one day and it was sunny two days, but I don't know. I passed out."

"You did die," Dot told her.

"I'm not dead!" Amy cried. "It feels like I'm dying. I'm so dry."

After much persuasion, Amy began to wonder if she might possibly have died. "Am I in heaven?" she asked.

"No, but we'll help you to get there."

"Oh, my ears hurt and my neck hurts and my throat is so dry...it's really very peaceful here, on the pine needles.

"I was scared. (She was using my mind to think that she had gotten scared about animals as she got weaker, so she had put herself in the brush to hide.)

"What if a bear came while I'm here?"

"You're dead, and I'm going to get you to heaven," Dot explained.

"Who are you?" Amy wondered.

"I'm here to help you."

"I can't have had a funeral 'cause I'm not dead yet! Will I have one when I die?"

"You don't know do you? You'll get all that information when you cross over."

"I don't know where I am...they won't find me when I die..I'm too well hidden 'cause I was afraid of bears and things. I got very lost. I didn't know which way to go and I just kept going and I never got out of here—and I'd slide."

Then Amy looked down and discovered my body.

"What do you see?" Dot asked.

"I don't see my body!"

"You're in spirit."

"This isn't my body."

"It's Shirley's," Dot said, trying to reassure her.

"Where's my body...I didn't die yet."

Dot finally was able to convince Amy to cross over. And what a surprise for her when both her parents, her high school sweetheart, her husband and her dog all came for her.

I could see her (myself) lying on the side of a hill when she first came through me. I could see what looked like the Muir Woods. After Amy crossed over, I told Dot that "the trees were tall, tall with sunlight shining through. She was in a lot of leaves on the slope. She had given up."

It's really quite difficult to persuade the spirit of a dead person to cross over if they do not know that they have died! But imagine what it must be like to convince someone who thinks that they are actually falling off a tall building, still living the sheer terror of the experience. Dot really had to work hard to cross over this spirit.

I was acting as the medium, and Dot as the interviewer, when a spirit voice suddenly cried out, "Ahhh! Oh! I'm falling!"

"You're not falling. You can sit up," Dot said, trying to

reassure the spirit who was writhing in horror in the wing chair in her living room.

"OH! OH!"

"Where did you fall?"

"Oh! Off a building. OH! Look at it down there. OH! OH! OH!" a male voice screamed. "I'm gonna die! I'm gonna die! I'm gonna die!"

"Yes, you did. You died. That's how you died. It's all over now. It's all over. You can sit up now and be comfortable," Dot said, as my body continued to move all around in the chair.

"I can see the ground!"

"It's okay. You can sit up now and be comfortable. It's all over."

"How can I sit up?" he demanded to know. "I'm falling through space!"

"Treat it like a dream. It's all over," Dot repeated, trying to reassure him.

"It isn't a dream! I was washing the windows!"

"Where was this?"

"Chicago. On the twenty-sixth floor!"

"Look at me," she commanded.

"What are you, an angel?" he asked. (It felt like my body was suspended in mid-air.)

"In a manner of speaking. I'm holding you."

"Where's your wings?" he challenged.

"Oh, they don't show," Dot replied. As the spirit continued

to clutch her hands and pull her arms painfully in all directions, she pleaded, "Don't twist my hands. Come on, come on. You're all right!"

"I'm gonna die! I'm telling you, I'm gonna die!"

"Don't worry about it. Tell me—"

"Why aren't I falling any faster? What's happening?"

"Because I'm holding you now. You're all right.

"What's you name?" Dot asked.

"Walter Muzursky."

"Don't look down. Walter—Walter, look at me!" Dot commanded.

"Wha-a-a-t? What, what, what?"

"Just look over here. How old are you, Walter?"

"Twenty-six."

"And what year is it?"

"1942."

"Okay. And what happened?"

Walter continued to sound very nervous as he seemed to think that he was still in the process of falling. "My safety strap bro-o-o-o-ke."

"And what building was this?"

"I don't know if it had a name. I'd just go to the address...it's gonna hurt when I land. I'm gonna be smashed to smithereens!"

"It's 1987. It's all over."

"You're just being nice."

"No, I'm not. It's all over. You're here with us now. You're safe," Dot assured him.

"I'm gonna be smashed to smithereeeeens!" he screeched in terror.

"It's all over. Whatever happened, it's all over," Dot told him.

"Help," he begged piteously.

"I'm helping you. It's all over..."

"I'm gonna die!" Walter said tearfully.

Finally he recognized that family members were coming for him from the other side. "My mother and Uncle George are here!" he said in surprise.

Dot thought Walter would break her arm before she got him crossed over, his grip was so strong and his emotions were so violent. And of course, as the medium, I had plenty of exercise in Dot's chair.

I asked my guide, Mary, why some people have a continuing experience when they die. "Some people have a continuing experience because that is all they know. Their mind is so disciplined that it cannot accept death," she replied. "Not the fact that they have died, but death itself. That is the reason for a CT (continuing experience) as you call it."

CHAPTER VIII

Ghosts

Some people will probably disagree with me when I say that I think ghosts are very unhappy spirits who are misbehaving for some particular reason. Their behavior could be extreme in our eyes, but they are so unhappy with their situation that it is the only way they know how to express themselves, even if it is with a vengeance. Some of their actions would be considered so despicable by us that we might tend to think of them as very evil beings. But because of the many ghosts I have helped to cross over I must state that I consider every one of them to have been unhappy, some extremely so; and not one of them would I consider to actually be evil. It seems that the more unhappy they are the more serious their actions appear to be.

I asked for this particular ghost to come because I had learned about her violent behavior from the author of a ghost book who had researched this case. I wanted to help her. She had actually tried to possess the body of a woman who had no idea what was happening. This spirit's behavior caused the woman to become so wild and unruly that she had to be restrained.

When we asked for the spirit to come to be Rescued, she did come. I was reminded of the wicked witch of the East in the *Wizard of Oz*, as the spirit came through me with a horrible screech, then laughter and the pounding of the chair, giving Ruth her initiation into the Rescue of ghosts.

"We can give you peace," Ruth said. "We can give you peace."

"Oh, wouldn't that be wonderful for all you people," the spirit snarled, and she began to laugh. "I don't want to cross over. I want to cause trouble. I love it!"

"What is your name?"

"What difference does it make? I am not going to go. I'm not going to go! I'M NOT GOING TO GO!" she screeched.

"How did you die?" Ruth inquired.

"I was there before all of them were there."

"Was it your house?"

"No, but there was something there before and it was mine!"

"And you'd like to have it back. Would you like to have it back?"

"Well, it was my property first!"

"So, that's what's bothering you?" Ruth asked.

"Of course!"

"You could be much, much happier. You could do good instead of evil. It would be just so much more fun."

"Ha, ha. I'm having fun as it is," the spirit retorted.

"You were born good, not evil. Think about it. And if the house—"

"You're just trying to convince me because you want to get rid of me. You don't want me to bother people anymore."

"I'm sorry for you."

"Why?" the spirit asked.

"Because you really aren't happy. You're lonely, and you could go back and plan the happiness you once had when you were a little girl...you could have unconditional love and you'd be forgiven for the mischief you caused...you could help people and you'd be happy."

The spirit began sobbing. "You're trying to hurt me," she said, and her voice began to sound less angry.

"No, I'm not. I'm trying to help you. Please don't be so sad." Ruth pleaded in a very sympathetic voice.

"...your mother loved you and your father loved you."

"No they didn't."

"You dreamed of having a mother who loved you."

"Yes—but they didn't."

"Maybe you just thought they didn't, but if you cross over...you'll be so happy and it will make up for all the sadness you had suffered as a little girl..."

"You didn't suffer like me! You weren't beaten!" the spirit shouted.

"You'll know love such as you can't even know on this earth. Love greater than a mother's love—just beautiful, beautiful love..."

"I HATE YOU!" the spirit screamed at the top of her lungs.

"I know. It's uncomfortable. You're forgiven for what you've done."

"I haven't done anything. It's my property!"

"It can still be your property in heaven. You can carry the rememberances of that house with you...think of it, you can—"

Again, the spirit became very upset, interrupting Ruth to scream, "But it's MY PROPERTY!"

"It'll always be your property. You can carry it with you to heaven and it'll be the dearest—" Ruth was searching for words to convince her. "You can build another place like it in heaven and live there all your life."

That must have struck home because the spirit began to cry—almost in desperation.

"You can have happiness such as you've never known before," Ruth continued.

"Why are you doing this to me?"

"Because I hate to see you suffer. You've suffered enough. Don't suffer anymore. Relax, and take the blessings that are waiting for you. You're loved. You're loved."

"What about the person that killed me?" the spirit inquired, thus giving Ruth one more problem to deal with.

"He has to learn. He has to have a learning experience, but he can't kill your spirit. Your spirit can be here and you can have joy that you've never known before."

"How do I know this is all gonna happen?"

"Come and stand here by my right side, and some kindly spirit who loves you will come and bring you peace and happiness and joy and help...you'll learn how to forgive even the person who killed you. He was a sick man. It shouldn't have happened. And your parents were sick and you'll learn to forgive them."

"I don't want to forgive anybody!" she cried out.

"Well, for now you just need to rest and be here and that will come later. But you certainly will be loved..."

"I didn't die young. I was twenty-six," the spirit said, in a calm voice, as she crossed over.

When this spirit, definitely defined as a ghost, was in my body, I could feel a very angry person. "I could feel the hate," I told Ruth.

One problem I have with those who rid buildings or areas of ghosts is that not all "ghostbusters" or exorcists attempt to cross over the spirit who is doing the haunting. This is a very sad state of affairs as the poor spirit will still have all the misery and suffering that caused it to be a ghost in the first place. And not only that, but if the ghost is forced out of one location, it will certainly have to find another location and may never be crossed over.

As ghosts are still on the earth plane, they still have earthly energy. This energy seems to have much more of a human feel to it. I can attest to that fact. Both my father-in-law and my uncle hit me at different times, and it felt just as though a real person was hitting me.

My father-in-law appeared on the scene the moment the family began to clean out my mother-in-law's house. He had been dead twenty-six years. Edna was no longer able to live in the house, and we were going to have to sell it. James let his presence be known by hitting and yelling. He was actually behaving as a ghost.

With my first partner, Dot, acting as the medium, I tried to cross him over.

"Leave me alone," the spirit voice said.

"Is that you, James? You haven't crossed over, have you?" I asked.

"Why don't you leave me alone? What difference does it make? I'm so sad." He sounded close to tears.

"Do you know," I asked, "that you're stuck on the earthly plane and that when Edna dies you'll still be stuck here?"

"We'll go together."

"No, it doesn't work that way, James," I said. "You can't go by yourself."

"I feel alive," James retorted.

"That's because you're stuck here. You didn't go to heaven when you died...that happens when people die if they don't cross over. Then they can't cross over by themselves. Have you tried to cross over by yourself?"

"Well, I'm not going anywhere!" he announced. "I love Edna...I'll go with her when she goes," he insisted. "I'll go with her."

"You won't be able to," I replied. "You have to go when you die...you're trying to behave like a person still and you aren't a person. You died twenty-six years ago. It's now 1986."

"That doesn't make any difference as long as my Edna is

here."

"What have you been doing?" I questioned.

"Hanging around," James replied.

"Why didn't you cross over when you died?"

"I didn't want to leave Edna down there in Texas," he said, referring to the location of his sudden death.

"How sad it will be for Edna that her own husband is not going to be there to welcome her when she goes."

"You mean we're not going to go together?" he asked.

"No, you're not," I replied. "That's not how it works. Maybe if you died in the exact same place at the exact same moment you'd go together, but you're already dead and you've been dead for twenty-six years. You already had your chance to go. We're giving you your second chance, and I hope you take it because it's going to be terribly sad for her when she goes, not to find you waiting for her."

James wanted things to be clarified. "Well, you're saying that even though I cross over, I can still come back?"

"Yes," I replied, quite exasperated by this time.

"Well, let me take a look. I don't guarantee I'll go. Let me take a look."

But James did cross over and is now on the spirit plane waiting for Edna.

My Uncle Martin, hit me on the arm when I opened his closet door. It felt like an actual person had hit me as there was so much energy in the force of the blow.

As most spirits don't cause trouble, few people know when there are spirits hanging around them. They do know when there are ghosts around though. We think of ghosts as a separate category of spirits and refer to them as ghosts simply because they are causing trouble. Ghosts may have particular people in mind when they are causing the trouble or they may just like to have it known to those in human form that they are around.

One ghost, in a castle in Switzerland, had been a spy from Milan. He was caught by the Duke of Savoy in 1544, and left to starve to death in the castle's dungeon.

"They tortured me," Luigi told Dot. "They tried to burn my feet. They chained my arms and my legs. They did not find anything out that they wanted to know, but they did not let me go because they did not feel comfortable.

"I didn't cross over because of VENGANCE!" he shouted.

"I didn't have a funeral. Thrown in a sack—in a hole in the ground..."

"You stayed around to haunt them? How did you?" Dot asked, trying not to display too much curiousity.

"Knocked goblets off the tables, tripped people, tipped chairs. Oh yes, I had a wonderful time!" Luigi said gleefully.

"Were they aware of these things being done supernaturally?"

"I think so. They tried to shoot me!" he said as he laughed heartily. "They knew a ghost was there. I don't know if I was visible to anyone, but they tried to shoot me.

"I knocked over the chairs when their attention would be on them—in a very carefully devised manner."

"How did you do that?"

"I tipped them slowly," he replied, as he laughed again.

"I had my vengance. I even rolled a cannon ball across the floor, across the castle floor! It was stored in the upper ramparts. It was easy. The floor was not even. Just gave it a little shove and it went across the floor...

"I think there was a big fire in the fireplace and they were sitting around after having eaten—well relaxed, but not for long 'cause I aimed it at the fireplace. But they retrieved it.

"I had my fun. I haunted the premises as long as the Duke of Savoy lived there and after, many years!"

Ghosts usually have a very emotional reason for hanging around and not crossing over. Therefore, it often takes the ghost several visits with us before we are able to convince him or her that it would be better to cross over rather than hang around on the earthly plane. Each time they come through me they are a little less emotional.

There are some ghosts, though, that are willing to cross over the very first time. No one has listened to their story. No one has shown any sympathy toward them. No one has offered any love. And no one has offered to cross them over! Luigi was one of these. He had come of his own volition, which was unusual, as most ghosts have to be called by us. And he was willing to cross over after he told Dot his story.

She forgot to ask him how he had found us, but it might have been a case of seeing me when I, myself, had visited a castle in Switzerland a few months prior to his Rescue.

Some ghosts will be haunting the house where they lived, or the building where they worked, or the place where they died, or the spot where they once lived even though their actual dwelling is no longer there. Some ghosts have been haunting the ground where they were buried because it has been disturbed. But many ghosts are simply where they are because they lived or died in the general area, and they are attracted to a particular building because one person or many persons in that building are psychic or interested in spirits or in ghosts.

That was George's explanation of why he was haunting a particular house in Maine.

"I know this house wasn't there," George said.

"Why did you pick this house to appear in?" Dot asked.

"Because," George explained, "it's right there in the area (where George was killed) where we were hunting the deer. It's right there in the woods. I never went in that house before."

"What brought you in this time?"

"Some kind of energy. I just felt attracted to it. There's something strange about that house."

"What do you mean?" Dot asked.

"I don't know." George found it difficult to explain. "There's more energy in that area than some places right around there. But we were hunting in the woods there. But just like here (referring to Shirley's living room), there's a lot of energy here—a lot of spirits. It's the same kind of energy."

"But the lady there isn't doing Rescue work," Dot informed him.

"That doesn't have anything to do with it," George answered. "If I feel attracted to some place..."

"Your wife is dead," Dot reminded him.

"Yes, but I would like to know if my death was an accident."

"You'll find out on the other side."

"I thought I'd find the answer in that house."

"But that house wasn't even there."

"But that lady's psychic or whatever you people call it," George replied.

I happen to know the lady who asked us to Rescue George and George is correct, the lady is psychic!

One family in Maine had at least three ghosts in their house and several more in the immediate area. One died there, and one died nearby but had visited there many times because a relative had owned the property. Several other ghosts were attracted to the house because the other spirits were already there, or so they told us.

Quite often we are asked to see if we can rid a particular home or building of whatever spirit or spirits are causing trouble. Most of the people making the request can tell us specifically what type of behavior is taking place. Many times the ghost will follow a predictable pattern of behavior, but this next one seems an exception.

Stanley is one of the few ghosts we have Rescued who wasn't called by us. I thought he had an unusual story to tell. When he came through me he commented about the other spirits waiting to be Rescued. "I guess we all must be behaving pretty bad...it's in the air, a full moon...it was beautiful last night," he said.

"What happened to you?" Dot asked.

"I drove into a tree. I was driving too fast. I can see my car with its rounded fenders. I can see it before it hit the tree."

"What year is it?"

"1942."

"How old are you?"

"Twenty-eight."

"Where were you?"

"I was home on leave from the Navy, at San Diego, for my father's funeral," he explained. "I was on a light destroyer...I had three brothers and one sister in the service."

"Why didn't you cross over when you died?"

"I wanted to see how the war came out."

"What did you do while you were waiting?"

"I went to the battles. Wow! It was exciting! Really exciting. See, I hadn't been in any battles when I was killed in the car accident. I had only been in San Diego a short while and we hadn't been out. I hadn't seen a single battle, so I went back."

"What did you do before you went in the Navy?"

"I worked in a defense plant and my company tried to keep me from being drafted because they claimed I had an important job, but I said, 'To Hell with that! I'm going in the service and that's that!' They weren't going to let me go!

"Anyway, I went to Kwajalein. I went to Iwo Jima. I went to Saipan. Oh, boy, I hit all these places! It was terrific!"

Dot was really surprised. "In spirit form?" she asked.

"What do you think, I made up a new body?"

"Did you do anything so anybody knew you were there, any of your old shipmates?"

"I don't think anybody knew I was there. It was all this excitement and tension. You had to be real quiet, so I was real quiet, too. I didn't bother anybody. Or, Rrrrrrrr," he said, making a sound simulating gunfire. "All the guns were going. Oh, gads. It was really something!

"You know what I did? I went over on one of the Japanese ships. It was fun."

"You didn't know what they were saying?"

"No, but I did things like this." And he gestured with his hand. "Gave them hits on the back of their necks and pinched their arms. Oh, yeah! Oh, yeah! A guy would be aiming a gun, you know, and I'd go 'ah, ah, ah' (indicating that he had poked someone in the midsection at a crucial moment). Oh, yeah. I did my share. It was really exciting. I wasn't going to miss this. I went out there and I was in the thick of things."

"So you made a real pest of yourself with the Japanese?"

"Yeah. I went to the Korean War, too...up hills, down hills. It wasn't the Navy. The Navy got them there. I tried going with them, but I didn't like it at all, so I said, 'To heck with that.'

"But I'll tell you the one I did not go to. I did not go to Vietnam. I saw it on the TV and I said, 'To heck with that.'"

"You didn't like that?" Dot wondered.

"Oh, every night they looked at it on the news. Oh, bad! That wasn't my type."

"You liked the sea battles?"

"Yeah, I like the battles out on the water, and I liked just people fighting against each other—not all these civilians dragged into it. It was too messy. I didn't like that. I was against it. It was interesting, but I watched in other people's living rooms. I wasn't going to go there.

"But that Pacific—that was really exciting. I really did my share. Oh, boy, there was many a gunner that missed his mark. They missed those American planes. Oh, brother! And, they couldn't understand why they would get jumpy at the last minute," Stanley said, as he happily recalled his adventures.

"There's no place I can go now to enjoy. I don't like what's going on in Lebanon and those Russians in Afghanistan! There's no place I can go to enjoy..."

"You're ready to go now," Dot stated, "so, let's do the process. Come over here and look straight ahead into the distance. It may be dark."

"There's a light. It's Louise."

"Who's Louise?"

"My girl friend!"

"Go with Louise," Dot instructed. And Stanley did. He crossed over.

When I am acting as a medium for Rescues, I know what the spirit is thinking. When Stanley was occupying my body he had had the thought that he didn't want to hang around any longer because there wasn't anything exciting going on in any ocean.

Once the spirit crosses over, the energy will be of a different nature. It seems to be more subtle, but it can be extremely powerful. The touch of a spirit who has not crossed over feels, to me, just like that of a person, but it has a softer feel if they are on the spiritual plane. This may not apply to others who have been touched by spirits.

Thus, if there are several ghosts in a building, it can be quite uncomfortable for the occupants. I can think of a few homes in particular which we have worked on which had several ghosts, and the amount of energy generated by these spirits was very uncomfortable.

In fact, there can be so much energy when we are doing Rescues that the tape recorder will actually be affected. It will sound like there is a tremendous amount of static. The static is so bad that it is difficult to hear what is being said on the tape. I even asked different engineers and sound technicians to tell me what was wrong with my tape recorder, but they couldn't explain it. It turned out to be spirit energy over which I had no control. There were just too many spirits waiting to be Rescued!

Just a few earthbound spirits in one location, with their type of energy, could attract other earthbound spirits in the area, my guide Mary told us. Mary also said, "There's been a lot of turmoil (referring to the spirit energy) because once it's in the air it accumulates." And that is what happened a number of times.

One home in particular is "clear" now, but it had the misfortune to be built on a Native American burial ground. The burial ground was there because the area had been the scene of an Indian massacre by whites and other Indians. And as we crossed the Indians over, one by one, more earthbound spirits in the area were attracted to the house and eventually we found we had crossed over more than forty spirits during a period of two years. Some spirits misbehaved in the extreme form by attacking one of the occupants of the house more than once. We considered them ghosts because of their behavior, but most were just hanging around and waiting to be helped.

Some people like having the ghosts around, but it is actually harmful for the ghosts in the long run because they may dissipate if they are on the earthly plane too long, and their spirits will be lost forever.

There is more than one place where I have volunteered to Rescue ghosts, and the owners have asked me not to as they liked having the ghosts. In one particular country inn the manager said that his ghosts brought in extra business on certain holidays. I knew he had them because they sat on my head while I ate my lunch there.

I also wonder if perhaps some people don't want anyone to Rescue their ghosts because these people think that there might be some kind of retribution. Perhaps they think the ghosts will come back and do something worse than they have already done—just because someone Rescued them, and they really didn't want to go.

One day Dot asked my guide, Mary, about the seeming absence of herself and Harry, Dot's guide, when we sat to do investigations of hauntings. It seemed as though on the days we did that, Mary and Harry were not around. "Is someone else stepping forward to oversee this sort of activity?" Dot asked.

"No," said Mary, "we are always there when you do this sort of work, but because the spirits that are not ready to cross over are more skittish, we do not want to cause them any more anxiety by being close. We do not want them to think that they are being forced to do anything against their will, so we do stay in the distance when you are working on hauntings."

I hope anyone reading this chapter will be happy to ask someone to Rescue any ghosts they might have so that the poor spirits can at long last have peace and happiness. The ghosts will think they do not want to cross over because they are having so much fun, but they do not realize how important it is that they do go to the spiritual plane. And, of course, there may be other reasons why they do not want to cross over such as fear of what lies beyond, or perhaps punishment for past deeds.

CHAPTER IX

Time To Cross Over

When we are ready to do an actual Rescue, my partner and I hold hands, and the energy of the spirit who is using me, as the medium, can be felt in our hands. We feel the energy leave our hands altogether as the spirit crosses over.

The spirit uses the mind and voice of the medium, so therefore, if the spirit speaks a foreign language there is no problem. Everything that is said will be in English. And in addition, since the spirit is using my mind, I can pick up and know whatever the spirit, who is in me, is thinking.

We ask the spirit to tell us his name, what year it is (which will be the year of death), his age, where he is (city and country), and something about himself, his family, and his work. The spirit remembers the last thing that happened to him and the last place he was in body. He usually doesn't know the present year, but he almost always seems to know where he is when we proceed with the Rescue—usually my house or my partner's house.

The spirit may know everything that has happened to him since death occurred or he may have felt like he was floating in a dark colored void, unable to understand where he was or what he was doing there.

Aranamus, the Roman soldier, whose spirit survived longer

than any I have ever helped to Rescue, told Ruth, "I have not known where I was. There has been nothing but a whirling black mass."

And, of course, the spirits have no concept of how long they have been dead. There is no concept of time except here on earth. So imagine how surprised they are when they find out how many years have passed since they died. Sometimes, it's hundreds!

The spirit may have tried to cross over, on its own, after having been earthbound for many years, and found that it was impossible to do so.

Bernardo was one of these. He died in 1573, in an area that is now part of Italy. He found it impossible to cross over when he was ready.

"What kept you earthbound for over four hundred years?" Dot asked.

"Well," replied Bernardo, "you can't go when you try, because I tried later...and I wasn't able."

"How did you try? What did you do?"

"Well, I just decided I was going to go—that there was no point in hanging around any longer, and, well, nothing happened. And I cried, 'Help, Momma! Help, Momma!' because I knew my mother had died.

"Nothing happened! No one helped me. But it doesn't seem like four hundred years, I must admit. Time must go awfully fast. It does not seem like that long a period of time."

Then the spirit is instructed to look for a light. That light will be the spirit of someone who has died and is on the spiritual plane, and who is coming to help the stranded spirit cross over. This welcoming spirit will be that of someone who loves the stranded spirit very much and has been waiting for it. The spirit wishing to be Rescued, as well as I, will see the welcoming spirit in the form of light. And when the earthbound spirit sees the light, it identifies who it is it sees without our asking. Sometimes the spirit knows who has come for it, but it does not see a light. It just knows who is there. When that is the case I do not see a light either, as I see whatever the spirit in me sees.

There is no age limit. The loving spirit may be that of a baby or a very old person, but usually it is an immediate family member who has come to help in the Rescue. There are also occasions when it is the spirit of a dear friend or a fiance'. Sometimes several spirits will come to help in the crossing over.

"Well," said Henry, "I guess I'd better go. My father's here and Aunt Millie and Uncle George are here, too, and my grandfather, Sam."

Another spirit with quite a welcoming committee was Frank who had died more than one hundred years ago, and who had three wives and seventeen children. We weren't surprised when so many loved ones came to help him.

"Are you ready to cross over now?" Dot asked.

"Yes," Frank answered, "because Nellie died."

"What were the names of your other wives?"

"Winnie and Martha."

"Maybe one will come to greet you," Dot suggested.

"Nellie come?"

"Yes, she'll probably be the first one.   I see you had a favorite."

"Well, she was my last one," he explained.

"Do you see a bright light?" Dot asked, referring to a spiritual presence.

"Winnie's here.   Everybody's here—even some of the babies are here!"

"Why are you crying, Frank?"

"I want my babies."

"Well, you're with them now."

"It's a happy day!"

Even pets come to help in the crossing over, but they are never alone. The spirit of a human being is always with them. It's truly a pleasant surprise for the spirit waiting to go.

This little girl's dog also came for her. She had died in 1937, leaving her mother, father, brother and dog.

"Spot was brown and white with more than one spot," Wendy told me.

"I didn't cross over because I was going to take care of Spot. He was going to miss me. I was the one who had to put his water down, let him in and out. I tried to take good care of him. Mommy said we couldn't have a dog unless I took care of him because she had the baby and it was my responsibility."

I asked Wendy to come and stand next to me and look for

the bright light. "Someone will be in the light who is coming to take you across to heaven," I told her.

"I've got the feeling they're all here—Mommy and Daddy and Spot...Spot is barking and wagging his tail!"

Whoever is acting as the medium will see what the spirit in them is seeing. That was true in this case.

Lou was only eleven when she died.

When she was ready to cross over I asked her who had come for her.

"I see my mother."

"Do you see anyone else?"

"I see my cat, Fluffy," she replied, laughing.

After Lou crossed over, Dot, who was the medium, told me, "I could see that Fluffy was black and white and part angora."

I told Dot that Lou had a lovely smile on her face when she saw her mother and her cat.

Sometimes I can see what the spirit looks like who is using my body. I don't know why I can't see them every time, but perhaps they are able to project themselves purposely so that I can see them. I can always see what they see when they are looking for other spirits who are waiting to cross over. Often they ask my partner if she can see them and once in a while she can.

And many times I have felt exactly the same physical feelings the spirit has felt just before he died. This is particularly so when the spirit is having a continuing experience, as I described earlier, and does not know that he has died.

But the physical feeling can also occur when the spirit knows that he has died. Water in the lungs, blows to the head, pains in the chest—all of these are sensations I have felt, as the spirit in me was experiencing them when they were in the process of dying.

The one good thing about these sensations is that they are not as painful as they would have been had the spirit been in a living body. Many spirits have told us that the pain was not as great when they were dying. I think that information is worth knowing for those of us who are still here. It should lessen the fear of death.

Many times we have been told by spirits who have come to be Rescued, that while they were ill, a relative in spirit did appear in their room. However, since nothing was said by the spirit, the sick person did not know the reason for the visit. No mention was made of crossing over at the time of death. Seldom has anyone who has had a sudden death told us of a similar experience.

When Dot interviewed my father five years after his death she asked him about this. "All right, Harry, let me ask you now, when did you first notice loved ones, or people you knew from the other side coming for you—at what point in the dying or death process?"

"I saw my mother before I died."

"At the hospital? And what did she say?"

"Nothing. I just saw her."

"And then—forward from there—"

"Then I didn't see anyone again until I crossed through the light."

In another interview we were able to find out about this spirit's final moments on the earthly plane. As a group of friends we had gathered round to talk to Edith, who had crossed over only four months earlier. She, too, died in a hospital. She had been ill for several months.

"Everything is known," Edith said. "There isn't any such thing as time—it was my time—I didn't realize how sick I was."

"Did you realize you were going to die?" Ruth asked.

"I think it's different with different people...I'd say I realized it almost at the end," Edith replied.

"I had a beautiful experience...the night before. I saw my mother at the foot of my bed...and I understand that's rather common to see someone that you love a short time before you yourself leave...it's like they're giving you a little hint...I mean they just come and they stand there and you feel good about it."

"Did you sense that it was a warning?"

"No, I thought, 'I'm having one of those mystical experiences.' But I think that everyone of you—when the time comes, you'll probably have the same thing happen to you—especially if you're sick—really sick."

Others coming to be Rescued have told us that the spirit of a relative appeared at the funeral, but they did not state their reason for being there, so the dead person's spirit did not realize that they were supposed to cross over with them.

I'm sure that if the spirits who appeared to those who were about to die, or had just died, would send the message that they had come to help in crossing them over, there would be a lot fewer spirits hanging around. Knowing that you are supposed to go and that a loved one is waiting to receive you might alleviate a lot of the fear that many spirits must feel. So is there a glitch in the system? I don't know the answer to that question, but personally I feel the necessity for a change, and I'm just little me in this great big universe.

Another point of view should be reported here as I am trying to keep an open mind, and although I have felt strongly about the possiblity of a glitch, my new partner, Ruth, is inclined to think that it could be a matter of free will. You are given your choice, and it is up to you to decide whether you wish to cross over or not. If that is the case, then I think a loving spirit should appear and tell the spirit of the deceased that although they have a choice in the matter, if they don't cross over at the time of death it may be impossible later on and the spirit will need help. Not only should that possibility be emphasized, but the spirit should also be informed of the fact that if too long a period of time ensues before crossing over the spirit may dissipate!

I asked my guide, Mary, to come and talk to me about this, but her own spiritual helpers came instead. They said that, "a spirit who loves them comes, when an illness is involved, because they are concerned and wish to come and appear, but they only appear to the one who is ill."

Furthermore, they stated, "We know that you think there is a so-called 'glitch' in the system and that the loved one should come and tell the spirit of the dying person that they should cross over. But if the spirit is open to all things the spirit will know they should cross over. There is a lot of emotion involved in many cases and the emotion may be for a totally different reason in each person. It hampers the natural process of crossing over and so therefore, we say to you, it is human—human foible, or human aspect, but it is human. It happens. Not everything in a system, and this is a system—not everything can be perfect. And yes, there are millions out there waiting to be crossed over!"

If the spirit's body has not been found, the spirit should still cross over. Their body was the house for their spirit in life, but it is not necessary after death. So hanging around, waiting for the body to be found, will just make it more difficult to cross over later on.

Also, knowing that if you don't go when you die or at your service, that you might wait too long and never be able to cross over, just might be incentive enough for spirits to cross over. I don't think that too many of us wish our spirits to just dissipate into the universe because we have waited too long. And as I have said, that is what my guide said would happen.

CHAPTER X

Saying Your Goodbyes

I have been asked about the necessity of a funeral or any type of service. Some people do not want to go through the bother, I suppose. But I wonder if they have given thought to the fact that not only does the spirit of the newly deceased body need to say goodbye, but the living friends and relatives need to say goodbye, also.

In order to go through the grief process for those still on earth, it seems that some sort of a service, or thought process, in the form of saying goodbye must occur.

I had a very beautiful letter from a woman I had met in Maine, who had talked to me about my Rescue work and my belief in the necessity to have a service in order to say goodbye. She wrote, "My mother passed into spirit...in spite of her failing health it was a shock to the family.

"During her wake and funeral, I recalled many times things you had said...at difficult times I thought about our conversations and told myself that we were just 'hosting' an occasion where Mom could say her goodbyes, thereby easing the end of her journey here and the beginning of her new journey. Believe me, that thought helped me 'keep it all together' many times."

The spirits of the newly deceased also have to say their

goodbyes. What better way to say them than at the funeral or memorial service. All their friends and relatives are there, paying their last respects, saying their goodbyes.

Very few spirits have told us that they don't know whether they had a service or not. The service is very important to them, but they want the service with their body in evidence or at least found!

Henry didn't lose his body, but he had to wait too long for the funeral. He was a young American artist who had lived in Paris in the early part of the 1900s.

When he came through, Dot asked him, "What is the last thing you remember?"

"Hmm. The last thing I remember is going down the incline with a beautiful woman."

"What incline?"

"The incline right there at Montmarte'. It's something like a little funicular."

"And something happened to the car?"

"I think so," Henry said, "because all of a sudden—WHAM! And I think my head just hit something...do you want to know why I didn't cross over?"

"Yes," answered Dot. "What held you back?"

"Well, part of the problem was that my body was in France." He sighed. "And by the time it got back to the states it was quite a bit later, and I really—at that point I didn't feel like going in (into the body) because it was so much later that—and so much had happened, that I just thought, well I'd missed something. I mean I stuck around with all those French authorities, and I kept going back and forth to see what was happening with my parents, and, oh, it was a long time."

"Did they come over to—"

"No," he interrupted, "because the French authorities told them not to. The consulate took care of it. They wired some money, but, it took—it was more than three weeks before they had my funeral. By that time so much had happened that I thought, 'Gee, I'm going to miss something.' So—"

Dot guessed. "So, you hung around."

"Mm, but I shouldn't have because then when I tried to go, I couldn't."

Some can't leave because there are unusual circumstances surrounding their death, or the funeral is not what they expected. Perhaps a special loved one did not attend the funeral. Not only can the living lose the body of the dead person, but the dead person's spirit can lose those who are living.

Reggie died during World War II, and when he came through, Dot asked him what he was doing.

"I'm just hanging around waiting, that's what I'm doing," he replied.

"Why are you hanging around? Why didn't you cross over at your funeral?"

"Well, it was a strange funeral. I was killed in the war and I didn't cross over then because I wanted to come back and see my wife and children. The problem was, I couldn't find my wife and children."

"Why not?" Dot asked.

"They had moved. I couldn't find them, so I didn't want to cross over."

"Did you have a regular funeral?"

"I had something. They waited a while looking for her, but they never found Ellie."

"Well, she was listed as your dependent. Wasn't she getting checks (from the government)?"

"Don't know what happened," he replied. "She moved. She evidently didn't leave a forwarding address."

"That's very strange."

"Yes. I didn't find her, so I couldn't just go.

"My parents had a service, but they had a hard time because they didn't know what to do, either. Nobody could find Ellie."

I have been told that all information is supposed to be available and can be picked up by spirits. Some spirits who have died and not crossed over, may just be so upset that they aren't able to find their loved ones—to pick up any information about them. That may have been what happened to Reggie.

Dot was curious about saying goodbye. One day when we were sitting together, my father voluntarily came through me. She decided that it was an excellent opportunity to make her inquiries.

She told my father, "I'm glad you came through because I've been wanting to ask some questions of people who have gone through the death experience in the direct fashion. Now, do you remember your funeral?"

"Yes. Which one?"

"You had two services?"

"Well, my wife had a small, quick service at the hospital because I gave my body to the medical school, but the big service at church was neat!"

After Harry had explained how he had left his body, Dot asked him more about his funeral. "So then you came back to observe the funeral."

"Mm—hmm."

"So then at the church you were the only one that bothered coming for that (from the other side)?"

"Well, I don't know if anyone else was there. I didn't see anyone. I was very busy though, watching what was happening. It was very interesting 'cause I didn't know so many people thought so much of me."

It was obvious that the funeral service really made him a very happy spirit, and everyone who wanted to was able to say goodbye through their eulogy.

One friend told about her teenage son who, before he had been killed in a motorcycle accident, had gone to visit each of his relatives. She did not realize until some time after his death that he had been saying his goodbyes, but he had been saying them before he died.

Another friend has talked about her father-in-law coming

to her bedroom on the night that he had died. Later, when she inquired about the time of his death, she was not surprised to learn that it was about the same time as his visit to her. Obviously he was saying his goodbyes.

This is not to be confused with the spirit of a loved one coming and standing by the bedside of an ill person. As I have mentioned earlier, that occurs because the spirit is concerned for his loved one who at the time is still living.

When we talked to Edith after she had crossed over she explained a little about her service. She, too, had crossed over before her funeral.

"Did you see anyone you knew before you died?"

"The night before I died I did see my mother," Edith replied. "I didn't tie it in with anything frankly. I almost thought it was a dream."

"What happened at the funeral?"

"Well, I found out some people wait 'til their funeral, but I didn't. But my mother came back with me. Actually it turned out that my mother was there in the front to welcome me and she came back with me.

"Sometimes many, many members of the family come back, but because I crossed over before my funeral just my mother came back."

"I wanted to go to your funeral, but I just couldn't," Ruth explained.

"Saying goodbye to a person mentally and lovingly is the

same thing," Edith replied. "After I crossed over I came back and made a special point of saying goodbye to everyone."

"Shirley said you came to church the Sunday I talked about you."

"She's right," Edith said. "I let her know so she'd tell you. You have to find somebody who knows what's happening so they can spread the word."

The spirit of the deceased apparently desires to be able to attend some sort of a service where all his loved ones will be in attendance so that they can say their goodbyes. But if while still alive, a person does decide he doesn't want a service, he should remember that those left behind still need some sort of a service for themselves, so that they can say goodbye and begin to get over their own grief.

CHAPTER XI

The Welcome

Apparently the spirits of many of those persons who had been considered clinically dead had actually traveled to the spiritual plane. Some books on the subject of near-death experiences describe people as saying they were in a very bright light or in the presence of a very bright being of light. Some people have described beautiful scenery, more beautiful than anything they have seen on earth. One person even spoke of an angel accompanying her.

In one book there were also many similar descriptions of darkness. Black voids, black valleys, and black tunnels were described by those who had come back from death. These accounts of dark places sound similar to what many spirits who didn't cross over described to us as their experience after death. But these spirits we Rescued continued to remain in the blackness, unable to do anything about it until they were able to find us.

I have spoken to two different people who have had near-death experiences. One said she found herself on the ceiling of the hospital room, feeling very light, and looking down at her body. She knew she had the choice of whether to go on from there or come back into her body.

The other person said that when she left the body she felt

very light and went through a gray tunnel which had light at the end.   But she found herself back in her hospital bed, regaining consciousness, before she got to the end of the tunnel.

It may be possible that each person who has a clinical death has a different experience based on his belief system, or put another way, based on his own reality.   His own reality being his own being, his own concepts.   And as a result of his own make-up, how he experiences things, how he reacts.

After going through the tunnel of light, in a natural crossing to the spiritual plane, the spirits of the deceased are met by their loved ones on the other side of the tunnel and greeted with "open arms".   This is the description given to me by every spirit I have questioned who did cross over at the time of their death.

My father happened to come through when we were finishing Rescues one day, and Dot wanted to ask him some questions about his actual crossing.

"At what point did you cross through the light?" she asked.

"When I left my body and it was lying there."

"At the hospital?"

"Yes."

"Beautiful," Dot said under her breath.

"And as I went through the light," he continued, "at the other end, as I was coming out, I could see who was there."

"So, your spirit went up into the light when it was time to leave the body?"

"Well, first I—like—floated up and then I—like—saw a

tunnel and just felt like I seemed drawn to the tunnel—bright light—went through this tunnel of bright light and as I came out, there were people I knew."

Several months after Edith died, a group of friends, having many unanswered questions, gathered to communicate with her. Edith was happy to respond. She did not mention the tunnel, but she did describe the bright light and her feelings.

"When I actually died, I suddenly felt light as a feather—just, oh, so happy. A wonderful feeling. It's like all cares are lifted from you—I really felt exhuberant—I felt so happy. Didn't remember pain, but was quite medicated.

"Then I found myself suddenly in this feather-like feeling. An exuberant feather, if there is such a thing. Wisked right through the air. The light was glorious, the feeling was glorious, and the music was glorious...everything is just beyond description. Well, there isn't any place you can compare it to here on earth, and your wonderful feeling combined with your wonderful reception—"

"Was it like a great party?" one friend asked.

"Well, I suppose you could call it like that—well, there wasn't a lot of champagne going around."

"Whom did you see?"

"I saw all my family who had gone before me. But the whole thing—just to see all these people, these spirits, as you are feeling so wonderful, seeing these colors and hearing this glorious music—the whole thing just harmonizes beautifully and if that's death, there's nothing to be afraid of!"

"Was the music a chorus?"

"I do not know. I cannot describe it. The music was different than I'm used to hearing," Edith explained that evening.

Not everyone has the same kind of wonderful, multimedia welcome.

When Dot's sister died, Dot was afraid she wouldn't cross over. Dot had leaned over the open casket and told her sister about the wonderful experiences she would have in heaven. What a surprise thank you. Her sister hit her! Then Dot talked about heaven in the eulogy and promised her sister a party in heaven, but her sister still did not cross over.

The following week we were sitting in Dot's living room doing Rescues when Dot told me the story about her sister's funeral. She expressed a deep concern for this sister. Dot was certain she had not crossed over. So, again, Dot promised that if she crossed over, she would have a party in heaven.

That did it! Her sister came, we crossed her over, and I saw the party in heaven as she was experiencing it, in the form of fantastic colors moving in beautiful motion as a giant wave across Dot's living room. I described it to Dot, and she was so happy!

Since Dot died, she has come back numerous times to talk about her death and the spiritual plane. One of her visits was to a classroom where I was speaking to a professor and a group of his students. She described her welcome to the spiritual plane.

"What about this beam of light? Did you have this

experience of going into the light?" the professor asked.

"It was a tunnel—a big tunnel."

"Isn't there some sort of light at the end of it?"

"The whole tunnel is light...yes, and you see yourself going through it. The whole tunnel is bright light, and at the end of it it's even brighter," Dot explained.

"And does this bright light at the end of it have a personality?"

"My relatives were there."

The professor was relating to the information various people had given who had had near-death experiences.

One time a man came to see me who wished to speak to his mother who was in spirit. When his mother came through me, she informed him that she had not crossed over because she had been afraid to go through the tunnel of light when she had died. He told me that his mother had always had claustrophobia, so, of course, this made sense as to the reason she had not crossed over.

Together we crossed his mother over, and I knew she didn't have to worry about the tunnel of light because when the spirit waits until sometime later, after death has occurred, and has to be Rescued, there will be no tunnel. But this is really a poor excuse for not crossing over at the time of death unless you have a bad case of claustrophobia like this woman did.

Those spirits who are Rescued by us do not have a tunnel to cross through. Instead, their loved ones, in the form of bright light, come for them. We ask them to look for a white light.

Usually it is small, but becomes larger as the spirit of the loved one who is coming for them approaches.

Sometimes the spirit of a pet animal will appear as well as the spirits of those who have already crossed over. The spirit we are Rescuing is always surprised to see their pet and extremely happy!

Most of the time the spirits who come are a bright white or yellow in color, but I have seen spirits in other colors such as orange and purple. I was told that purple was of a higher level in the spirit world.

I have also seen a black outline around the bright light of some welcoming spirits. It was usually in the shape of a diamond or a square. Several times this was the indication that the spirit was that of a baby.

More than once I have seen a rainbow and those seemed like very special Rescues to me. One rainbow appeared when we were helping Sammy, our very frightened leprechaun. He could see it and I could see it, also.

Once in a while I'd hear music in the distance just as the spirit was ready to cross over. Each time we were told by the spirit who was being Rescued that it was the angels singing. The spirit who was crossing needed that assistance. Like the Bible says, "Ask and you shall be given," and they had asked!

Chapter XII

The Spirit Plane

I have communicated with many spirits on the spiritual plane either through automatic writing, or by letting them come through as I channel them when acting as a medium. They answer my questions while the tape recorder records what they say. Sometimes I write the questions down so that I'll remember what I asked when I listen to the tape later.

If someone is around who will ask the questions, I turn the tape recorder on and let the spirit answer. Of course, there are times when a friend or relative or just a friendly spirit will want to come through and talk to whoever is with me. I let that happen also, as there is always interesting information to be received from the spirit world.

This information from spirit is very helpful in convincing those poor souls who are reluctant to leave the earth that they must cross over. Many of them seem to need a great deal of reassurance before they are willing to take the chance. They have forgotten that they have probably crossed over before, some of them many times. It is the immediate situation that they are engrossed in now and possibly a very emotional one.

I can honestly say that all the information from those in spirit has really helped me as much as those I assist. I have learned how to handle certain situations better, especially those Rescues involving ghosts. My guide, Mary, has answered any questions we might have, and each time we sit to do Rescues she has come and spoken to us, thus giving reassurance that she is there as usual. Many times she has voluntarily given us explanations or advice. And, of course, it is absolutely fascinating to hear all about what is in store for all of us in the future. My knowledge has grown by leaps and bounds.

It's been wonderful to talk to those we once knew here on earth. We know them still and they know us. They are able to help us in our journey by giving us valuable information concerning their spiritual lives.

Edith's explanation of the spirit plane was revealing.

"Are you happy there?" one of the group asked.

"Oh, yes, friends and relatives."

"What are you doing?"

"I'm not doing a thing. I'm just relaxing and enjoying being with my friends and family. I found I needed a rest."

When someone asked Edith if it was all right to come back after crossing over and visit, she answered, "If you hang around too much and the person doesn't know, you can become a burden to their recovery (from your death). If you come and you prearranged it that's one thing, but if you come around and are with your family too much, it's very difficult for them to get over your death."

Edith, who had been English in her last life, said, "I seem to be quite English. I keep meeting all these English spirits. I don't know if that's typical or not..."

"What age are you—over there? What age did you choose to be?"

"There isn't any age you choose. It's how you are perceived by others—not spirits really—earthlings."

"What are you doing?"

"I am doing nothing—I am just relaxing...I am seeing old friends—mostly family members from when I was a lot younger, but it is the same as you imagine.

"It's very difficult, I think, when I think about it now...to explain. If someone had tried to explain when I was alive what it was like over here, I don't think I would have understood. I would have pictured it my way, not their way. I think it's very hard to explain what it's like over here...I think there's too much television and movies. Well, there's too many things that have been said that are incorrect...what happens in your life and what happened to you in previous lives—that's all there in your life."

"When you go over and you leave someone behind, what kind of love can you feel for the earthly person?" Patty asked.

"Oh, you can feel just the same.

"I still feel very human. I still feel like myself. I still have the same feelings I did have. I still feel like a person...the loved ones who have been already over here a long time—they still seem to me like the same people I knew.

"I think if I became someone else...this life would only be a small part of me then because I would be someone else. Meantime I am still me.

"I don't feel like I've been here very long at all...so, it's been mostly love and do you remember."

Patty wanted to know what Edith had chosen to do next.

"I haven't chosen to do anything. I'm just with my family and I'm enjoying it."

"Do you communicate with the mind?" someone else asked.

"Yes, it's all mental.

"If I came back I would use my own body so that you would recognize me," Edith explained. "I would appear to you as you want me to appear to you.

"It's really quite different over there. The thing is you've all been there before. You just don't remember it."

"When did you become aware you'd been there before?" Dot asked.

"I think after I arrived. The feeling is quite different. The feeling isn't a physical feeling—it's—I know I wouldn't be able to explain this if I said it, but 'the rhythm of the soul'."

Ruth asked if the mind survived. "It must," Ruth stated speculatively.

"Scientists have a lot to learn yet," Edith answered.

"You didn't relive your life through flashes, regretting certain things and being happy about other things?" Patty asked.

"As I understand that from what I have read, that is called a 'near-death experience' and those people came back."

"What do you remember when you were dying?"

"I don't remember. I remember my mother. That's the only thing I remember...perhaps all the pain and suffering— perhaps everything is blotted out. I don't remember anything.

"I know that if I wanted to, I could know what everyone was thinking, but I do not want to know."

"Do you know what people on earth are thinking?"

"No, but I know when someone thinks of me—I don't believe in everyone trying to find out what everyone knows."

"You do get a feeling of love from people here who think of you with love and remembrance?"

"Oh, yes, all thoughts are out there."

"So you were ready?"

"I was just ready to go and went."

Ruth said, "I felt guilty about not contacting you before you died."

"I have heard this before, these people that feel guilty after someone leaves, and there's no reason to feel guilty. That's part of the human element. Feeling guilty is a great thing. If you feel guilty you will feel better!"

Someone else wondered about a future life when there are so many people. "Where would they go?"

"There's a great deal of mass here," Edith said. "I am just a tiny, tiny bit of it. It is true it is endless, but there is more to it than you people realize.

"I think it's a wonderful idea to be working on yourself...I think I was so busy doing everything that I did not do for myself, and I think that you usually don't find it out until you're over here where I am.

"I'm just a novice at this—a repeat novice as you all will be—a repeat and repeat and repeat."

This conversation with Edith made us all feel great about crossing over. We were so glad to receive all this information first hand. It's much more convincing when you can talk directly to a spirit who has experienced the things that all of us want to know about.

I have gotten the impression that it is not at all unusual to feel guilty, for some reason or other, after a loved one dies. I have heard many surviving spouses talk about this. I heard one person say they were feeling guilty because they had not been at their loved one's bedside when he died. I heard another person say they felt guilty because they had been sick when their husband needed their help. And I, myself, had felt guilty when my neighbor, who was a widower, had been found dead, because I felt that I had not done enough for him after his wife died. But I was lucky, because he came and told me through a spiritualist minister that I should not feel guilty about that. That was a wonderful experience.

About three weeks after Dot, my first partner, had crossed over, some friends and I got together to talk about our feelings of loss. Dot came through me and began telling the group just what she was doing. She didn't really want to talk to anyone at that time. She said she was resting and would be for a while.

This is not unusual. Many people who have come to see me, because they wished to speak to their loved ones in spirit, have told me that the spirit was still resting and really didn't want to talk to them. The average period of rest appears to be about three months, in our time frame, but many spirits have said that it depends on how much rest the spirit actually needs. Those with a traumatic death seem to need a longer rest.

Three months later I was speaking to a class of philosophy students when Dot unexpectedly appeared. After lecturing about Rescues, the professor and I did a Rescue. Then I wanted the students to be able to ask questions of someone who had crossed over, so I asked for someone, in spirit, to come through me and talk about what it was like on the spiritual plane. I said I preferred someone I had known in life.

Having done Rescues with me every week for three and one-half years, I was very pleased when it was Dot who came to talk to the students.

"Oh, oh. I made it," Dot said.

"May I ask who we have the pleasure of speaking to?" the professor asked.

"I'm Shirley's partner. I have not wished to speak before this. I just spoke with my friends a short time after I crossed over."

"What have you been doing?" the professor asked.

"I've been resting, but I'm not anymore," she replied.

"What do you see (over there)?" a student asked.

"It depends what I want to see."

"How do you feel?" the professor asked.

"I am feeling good because that is how I want to feel, because I didn't feel good. I felt terrible in the hospital. It was a horrible experience, and so, I want to feel good, so I am feeling good. You can feel how you want to feel."

Someone asked Dot if there was a landscape.

"If I want a landscape, I can have it, but I don't...right now. I am seeing all my friends and relatives over here because I have just finished resting."

"Have you been studying?" a student asked.

"No, I just got here. First you have to rest. Everyone rests."

"Then what happens?"

"They said I have to look at my records and find out what I am going to do, but they said there's no rush. A group of guides said I would have to do that sooner or later, but there's no rush.

"I can do what I want to do now and I don't know what I want to do yet. I think I'd like to find out more about things over here and the universe. There's so much that we don't know."

"Do you see yourself as having a body now?"

Dot laughed. "Not this body, no, no! But you can if you want to. You can present yourself as you used to look to a spirit or to someone here on earth."

"You recognize each other in some other way, I guess?"

"Oh, it's hard to explain...if you want to, you can look like yourself, and when you meet others you can have them look like you want them to look. In other words, if they are not thinking about how you want them to look because they have to pick it up—my thoughts, if I want to see them in human form, I can picture them instantly. It's really nice."

"Do you ever wish you were back on the other side?" she was asked.

"No, I don't want to go through that again."

"Do you know anyone who is not happy on that side?"

"I have not met that many yet. I have seen my friends and relatives and I have been resting, but I hope to meet more people—or spirits, 'cause when we did Rescues I used to tell them that when they crossed over, if they were interested in something— like there was a man who was an artist, who was haunting a house and he wouldn't leave. He told us that the minister who wanted to live in that house would have to hang each of his pictures in a room so that every room in the house had one of his paintings in it. And I thought if he crossed over then he could see the famous masters and he heard me and he came and went—just like that! So, you can see who you want to see.

"And, not only that, a friend of Shirley's said that his wife said that she went to a concert that Mendelssohn conducted. Imagine, Mendolssohn conducted a symphony orchestra in heaven! (Dot heard this said, after she had died, when she joined me at a conference I was attending.) So, I'm looking forward to a lot of these things."

"How do you live?" asked a student.

"You don't live. You just exist. You don't need anything. I don't even know how long I've been here. It feels like I just got here."

"And your family?" she was asked.

"I go to see them. I go to see them."

"Are they aware of your presence?"

"Oh, yes," Dot replied.

"Are you aware of what's going on in the world?"

"Oh, yes. I like to know what's going on!"

"What's it like there?"

"It's nice here. I feel at peace finally...I have just stopped resting and I am ready to go."

"What's resting?" another student asked.

"The spirit does nothing. It just stays in place--almost like sleeping. It's almost like sleeping. And it isn't the same for everyone though. Some rest for what you would call years."

"How do you feel?"

"I feel wonderful being here."

"Do you feel any particular age at the moment?"

"No," Dot answered, "but, I have a great load lifted off my shoulders."

"How did you happen to come here today?"

"I rushed right in as soon as she (Shirley) did this as I wanted to get right in here."

"Did you like doing Rescues?"

"The Rescue work was very satisfying."

"What do you call the place where you are?"

"Spirit World," Dot said.

"I understand you can think things into existence there. Have you tried doing that yet?" the professor asked.

"You can do that on earth," she stated. "Do you know that?"

"Have you tried doing that?"

"No, because all you have to do is wish what you want to be and it is," answered Dot, and she left!

Now at this point I feel I have to be honest about what I have found out about the spiritual plane through personal contact with others on that plane.

One day I happened to be looking through an old issue of *a* magazine and came upon an article which really surprised me. It stated that some spirits on the spiritual plane are not happy. These particular spirits were all well known when they were on earth, and they professed to be unhappy on the spiritual plane, and so stated through automatic writing to one single indiviual.

I had felt all along that everything that happens here on earth to each of us, whether it is good, bad or indifferent, is based on our own reality—how we perceive the event. It goes back to the theory of what is a concept. We are all different and so, therefore, our concept of something will not be exactly the same as the next person's concept of that same thing. Our concept will be formed based on everything that we have experienced. We make our lives what they are. We make our own beliefs. We make our own results. So it stands to reason, we make our own reality.

And the other point, of course, is that life on the spiritual plane is whatever we want it to be. We make it for ourselves, because we are making our own reality based on what we believe it will be like, or what it should be like. I guess you could say we do it to ourselves.

I decided that I would act as a medium and ask the spirits of people I had known, who did not seem to be happy on earth, to come through me and talk about how they felt on the spiritual plane. I would turn on the tape recorder and everything that they said would be recorded.

In fact, I thought that one of these spirits did have a negative personality here on earth. I took my chances on the response I would get, but in taping what was said, I knew that I would be able to listen to it afterward and form my own opinion.

The first spirit to come through was a surprise to me as I had not asked for him, but he had a very interesting viewpoint. We had been casual friends in high school.

"I didn't expect that it would be a great place and it isn't," John said. "I'm not happy here. Of course, I didn't think that I'd be happy here.

"You probably wonder why. Because I never really believed in the place. I didn't believe in anything. My parents were very confusing, so naturally I was confused. They didn't set me on any straight course—not that there's any straight course to set on. So, I thought there was no such place as this place, but there is actually a place (and he laughed) except it is not as it is conceived by many. It is not beautiful. It is not exciting. Does not make you feel peaceful. And it is definitely not the place for me, but here I am.

"Now I know what you've been thinking. You've been thinking that if a person thinks negatively about it—isn't going to like it or at least thinks they aren't, then that's exactly what happens—they don't like it.

"Well, I don't know if that's true or not, but I know I don't like it. There isn't anything that I can say I've enjoyed. There's a lot of negativity around me," John explained.

"You didn't know that I was a negative person. You didn't know me that way...but I was never happy about things...

"And I never really thought much about what would happen when I died until when I was just about to die—and then I had lots of negative thoughts—but I had lots of negative thoughts about my life long before that—and I honestly didn't expect anything over here and there isn't anything worth talking about. It's dull, dismal, negative—just what I expected.

"And so you'll be glad to put this in your report. It's a totally different viewpoint—totally. And, maybe you won't be glad to put it in, but at any rate I wanted you to know—there are many over here who know what is happening there.

"If you want to know something you can know something. I must admit that. But everything that's going on in the earth is just as bad as over here...and I know about your thoughts about creating your own reality. Well, perhaps that's what I did over here, but if I did it, somebody should have warned me 'cause I don't like it. And, I hope to get out of here one of these days.

"So you can put all that in your book. It won't make people feel great about coming here though. It might ruin your viewpoint—might ruin their viewpoint. Might ruin your whole book—who knows.

"At any rate, your friend, John."

John stated that he didn't think it "would be a great place" and he didn't think that he'd "be happy there." Well, my feeling is that he got his wish. He prepared himself, by his attitude, for the type of existence he would have on the spiritual plane. You might say he asked for it.

Perhaps if he had been more neutral or open to whatever he would experience, he would be having a much more pleasant experience.

Based on what Dot and Edith said about their attitudes and experiences in spirit, I would surmise that if John wanted things to be more pleasant they would be. It's almost as though he is telling himself, "I told you so."

The next person who came through to talk about his negative feelings was a relative I had asked for, whose viewpoint had always seemed to me to be quite negative. There never seemed to be a bright side to any event.

"This is stupid. I'd rather write a letter to you. I only like to talk when I feel like talking. I don't feel like talking. I don't know why I have to. I know what you want. I don't know what to tell you because I am aggravated still," Harry said.

"Resting is supposed to make you feel better. I don't know if resting made me feel better. I feel aggravated. Not this beautiful, warm, lustrous place that you say it is. I feel very antagonistic. I feel very antagonized. I wish I could be antagonized into action, but what kind of action a person can do here is beyond me.

"Yes, this is your father as you know. I'm not going to volunteer to do this again—to come when you ask. I don't like it. I don't like to tell you how I really feel.

"I didn't really want to come. I didn't think it would be so wonderful. Nothing wonderful has happened to me. What wonderful thing is supposed to happen I don't know because I'm just sitting around and doing nothing. They could sit...nobody suggests what I could do. They say it's up to me." He laughed.

"I'm just stuck here—watching what's going on—doing nothing. Don't know what to do. Whole thing is annoying.

"Now I suppose you want to know why it's annoying...at any rate, I don't know what I expect over here, but I'm not too pleased with the place. I think it could have a lot of improvement. I wouldn't even know who to tell that to. Some of them are so nice it's sickening. Now you may really wonder.

"I suppose you put all of this in your book? People might as well know the truth. It's not all goodness and light over here. There's messy situations. I feel very crowded in. I'm not sure what

I want to do, but I'm not doing anything I don't like. What I'm doing—which is nothing. That makes sense!

"I know you're thinking I'm still angry. Well, that's true. But I haven't had to see or deal with the people that I was angry with, and I heard some of the things people said about me.

"They think once you're gone you're not going to know what they're talking about. Well, I hear—if I want to and there's plenty I heard. Not all good. And not all bad.

"I don't know what you want to know. About the only thing I have is the sun rising in the morning. I like that. And, sometimes I have a big breakfast, but other than that I like it dark. You'd probably say 'dark and gloomy'. I don't know.

"Anyway, I'm not overjoyed by the place...this is what you wanted. You got it."

These two negative reports did dampen my enthusiasm, but only temporarily. I still believe in the premise of making our own reality; that we can have what we want to have when we cross over. If some spirits want to continue being miserable and unhappy like they were on earth, then evidently they can continue to do so.

Six months after Dot had first spoken to the philosophy students, she again appeared at one of my lectures, but this time to another group of students. She again spoke about her spiritual existence in the spirit world, as she called it. You might call this a continuing saga as she was now able to relate even more knowledge and experience.

"Well, let me tell everybody, I'm using her voice so it sounds like her, but I'm not using her mind if I can help it," Dot explained to the students. "I feel like I can have a mind of my own still, and I feel wonderful about that body—just wonderful."

"What do you have to tell us about today?" the professor asked? "Have you been exploring the afterlife?"

"Oh, yes, yes! Now I know more than I did."

When a student asked if Dot had seen any famous people walking around, she laughed.

"Walking around? You're only walking around if you picture yourself being human again—to some other spirit you know."

"How do you recognize them?" the student inquired.

"Oh, you know the ones you knew before, but if you want to look like yourself to talk to them—because sometimes that's fun."

"Is there a hell?" another student asked.

"I don't believe in hell. I think you make your own hell on earth. Everybody comes over here. When we did Rescues, because I was Shirley's partner, that's what we seemed to find out—that everyone comes over here."

"Is it the case, as we've been told, that you can think things into existence over there?" the professor asked.

"You can on earth, too."

"Doesn't it happen more or less immediately over there?"

"Well," Dot replied, "you have to be wise about it, but if

you want a beautiful day, gorgeous mountains, pretend you're in Switzerland—well—West Germany was my favorite. Well, here I am in the Black Forest."

"You just think that up?"

"Yes, and it's prettier than it actually was."

The professor was curious and wanted to know more. "I suppose you get information more directly than through the library."

"Oh, yes, you can take wonderful courses. Oh, you can find out about the whole universe, about man's total existence, about what's to come—anything you want!"

"Have you been taking any of those yet?"

"No!" Dot exclaimed. "I'm still—well, I just got here...I did seek out Lincoln. I've been looking around and I had to look at my record and—"

"Was Lincoln glad to see you? Is he bothered by many people calling on him?"

"No, no, he knew who I was, and he knew what I was thinking. We all know what each other is thinking. It's no problem at all. You just think it and you get the thought answer back."

"I gather you're happy there?" the professor inquired.

"Oh, yes. I feel so much lighter. It's wonderful."

"Now, do you have anything like eating or sleeping?"

"No, you just sleep in the beginning, for as long as you need it."

"Is there any companionship?" a student wondered. "Like spirits hanging around together?"

"If you wanted to, and if you want to be with your relatives you can be with your relatives."

After some additional questions, Dot gave this advice, "Well, my message to everybody is, 'Go when you die. Don't hang around.'"

One student asked, "Couples who die together—will they see the light together?"

"It all depends. I can answer that. If they want it they'll go together, but sometimes one person will hold back a whole group. In other words, if one person is afraid to go, sometimes the rest don't go either. Just because they all feel that it happened to them together and they have communion in spirit, so to speak.

"When the spirits come over here and they have a choice, then they see things in a very beautiful way. And they're shown their life, and the colors are beautiful, and everything stays that way while they're making their decision," Dot explained. "But, if you come over here...you know you're supposed to be here. And you are told just a little bit and immediately told to rest, and when you're resting you don't know anything..."

"When you then get through resting do you find it's like the near-death experiences that have been described? Is it still as lovely?" the professor asked.

"No, they aren't making it. It's made for them," she replied. "We can make whatever we want."

"Oh, I see. It's like all the travel posters. They give you the propaganda of what it's like over there."

"Not exactly, but you're close," Dot said, as she laughed.

"In other words, it's a standard picture they present to people."

"It makes them feel good in making their decision."

"Once they've decided to stay or come back again, then their life is what they make it."

"Yes," Dot replied. "After they've rested. You have to rest first—very important."

"I suppose the moral is to cultivate a positive attitude here and there. The more positive you are the more lovely the surroundings are?"

"No. Like I said before, I loved Germany and the Black Forest, so if I want to feel good and see it again, I don't have to go there to see it. I can just wish it and it's here. Not only that, it's more beautiful than it is on earth. The color here's even more beautiful than it is on earth."

"You have seen it on earth though, so you didn't conjure up a duplicate of it?"

"Any place I haven't been. If I wanted to pretend some place I hadn't even been to, I could come back to earth to that place. It's better than the equivalent on earth. It's more beautiful, and it doesn't have all the clutter and the people."

"Can someone who has died look down and see what I am doing?" another student asked.

"They can just come and visit you. It isn't look down...it's all around, practically...the transition between the spiritual plane and the earthly plane—there's a kind of a change in the energy field, but once you're here you can go into the earth energy field as often as you want—go back and forth—and you don't have a problem. So, you can be around whoever you want to be around any time."

"Where's the better place?" the student asked.

"Oh, here, here! Not on earth!" Dot responded with great enthusiasm.

"Do most people over there spend much time paying attention to what's going on here on earth?"

"I don't know. Depends on whether you want to or not. If you're still attached to your family."

The professor asked Dot, "How long have you been around? Did you find out when you looked back into your past incarnations; how many thousands of years or how many incarnations?"

"No, I've gone back about four hundred years. That's enough for now...they don't throw it all at you before you rest either. They just tell you a little bit, at least for me. I can't speak for everybody else because I haven't asked those questions."

"Now, do you have it planned out who your parents are? Is this something you work out with them?"

"Oh, yes, before you're born you work all that out."

"Is there anything you would like to share with us in terms

of practical lessons, in addition to go into the light and go across when the opportunity comes?" the professor inquired. "Don't hang around here?"

Dot replied, "But the other thing is, if you've got a problem with somebody, try to work it out while you're here because if you don't you have to come back and work it out all over again..."

"Well," the professor asked, "most people do, don't they?"

"No. Lots of people work the problems out."

"Then they don't have to come back?"

"Not to work out that problem again. That's why a person should never commit suicide, because if you commit suicide, you've got to come back and go through that whole type of a life again!"

"Would they be in this place again?" a student wondered.

"If they were perfect they wouldn't be in this place—you work your way up."

"Well, do some people work things out well enough that they don't have to come back here? Is that the case?"

"Yes," Dot replied, as she ended her own informative session.

I, myself, plan to be happy and enjoy myself, and have a beautiful time when I go to the spiritual plane. It will be my own reality making it so. It appears that it will be up to each of us to make his or her own reality, so there is nothing to be afraid of and much to look forward to. It is just up to each of us to decide what it is we so desire when we arrive.

I do feel, though, that it is of the utmost importance to get the message out to all people here on earth, that they must say their goodbyes to their families and friends, and cross over to the spiritual plane when they die. They will be able to go back and forth between the spiritual plane and the earthly plane as often as they wish once they have crossed over. Their physical ailments will be gone. They will have the chance to be happier. They will be able to have things as they so desire, but the spirit must cross over first! So, say your goodbyes and cross over. Don't wait to be Rescued!

THE END